THE MissADVentures OF A HAPLESS ENTREPRENEUR

TIMING IS EVERYTHING

Lessons from personal experience at the forefront of 21 extraordinary commercial and not-for-profit projects in Australia and internationally

Peter J Snow OAM

Timing is Everything | Peter J Snow OAM

First published in 2025 by BeInspiredBooks.com
on behalf of Peter J Snow OAM

© Peter J Snow OAM 2025

The moral rights of the author have been asserted

All rights reserved. Except as permitted under the *Australian CopyrightAct1968*

(for example, a fair dealing for the purposes of study, research, criticism or review), no part of this book may be reproduced, stored in a retrieval system, communicated or transmitted in any form or by any means without prior written permission.

All inquiries should be made to the author.

Creator: Snow, Peter, author.

Title: The MissADVentures of a Hapless Entrepreneur – Timing is Everything/ Peter J Snow OAM.

ISBN: 978-0-6487820-4-9 (Paperback)

ISBN: 978-0-6487820-3-2 (PDF version)

ISBN: 978-0-6487820-2-5 (ePub)

ISBN: 978-0-6487820-8-7 (Kindle)

ISBN: 978-0-6487820-7-0 (Audiobook)

Subject: Lessons from pioneering and innovative commercial and community impact projects conducted in Australia and internationally Aspirational, Inspirational and Motivational.

A catalogue record for this book is available from the National Library of Australia

Paperback Printed by: IngramSpark
Publisher: BeInspiredBooks.com
Project management: Community & Corporate Marketing and Public Relations
Cover design by 100 Covers
Cover photo by Ian Ritchie

Disclaimer

The material in this publication is of the nature of general comment only and does not represent professional advice. It is not intended to provide specific guidance for particular circumstances and it should not be relied on as the basis for any decision to take action or not take action on any matter which it covers. Readers should obtain professional advice where appropriate, before making any such decision.

To the maximum extent permitted by law, the author and publisher disclaim all responsibility and liability to any person, arising directly or indirectly from any person taking or not taking action based on the information in this publication.

Dedication

This book is dedicated:

Firstly, to JCI (formerly Jaycees International) for the skills, confidence and friends it has given me. It has changed my life and values for the better and given me a true understanding of purpose and community. Hopefully, I have at least partially repaid that gift.

Secondly, to my various business partners. financial backers and believers who have shared many adventures described in this book and made or lost money through them- and especially:
  (a) Bruce Gallash, a visionary extraordinaire and more than just a good friend with whom the ride has been bumpy but exciting;
  (b) Sciona Browne without whom my role with Albany's Historic Whaling Station project would have been far more limited;
  (c) Garry Leighton my much-respected predecessor as Chairman of the Jaycees Community Foundation with whom I shared commercial pain and 50-year friendship;
  (d) All Foundation Board Members past and present.

Thirdly, to my six grandchildren, Jack, Ashleigh, Karly, Sophie, Riley and Charlie (who destiny determined we would not meet in this life). Without working on a photobook for each of them so that they have some memories when I am no longer here to share them, this book would probably never have been written.

Timing is Everything | Peter J Snow OAM

FOREWORD

There is nothing more powerful than an idea whose time has come — Victor Hugo.

This book is all about great ideas — some successes and even some failures. However, it is also a testament to turning an idea into a categorical learning experience and in many instances, amazing experiences and successes. As the sub-title says: *timing is everything.*

It has been a joy for me to share in just a very small way, the journey of the author Peter Snow OAM. As members of the Junior Chamber International (JCI) organisation, we both had ideas and opportunities given to us. As the entrepreneur he is, Peter not only seized so many of the opportunities which came his way but created an amazing life story for himself.

As a visitor to the Whaleworld project in 1983 and then some 20 years later, I saw an example of how success follows an idea, hard work and perseverance.

How can one man do so much in one lifetime (which isn't finished yet)? How can one man visualise the prospects of an idea so incredibly well? And how can one man take others on his journey, so they too can share the experiences and learn in life?

The author could be called a teacher, a visionary, an entrepreneur (and so much more), but most of all he is an achiever. How many others would follow their ideas to fruition (and the occasional failure) and come out smiling and positive about everything tried, as well as being ready to embark on the next challenge?

What a way to learn. And that is what this book offers the reader. So many wonderful stories of taking opportunities, creating amazing results and showing that *impossible dreams are possible.*

Timing is Everything | Peter J Snow OAM

There would be times, some would not try for fear of failure. Failure, however, can be a great learning tool and creates valuable experiences and skills. And that is just one of the messages, for the reader of this manuscript.

Turning negatives into positives may not be easy, but it is a valuable skill to possess. It isn't easy, but enjoying the successes makes it worthwhile.

The variety of ideas Peter faced many times, shows determination beyond measure – accomplishments and fulfillment of life's meaning, showing a capacity to thrive even with difficulties.

As a graduate of the University of Life, the author has learned countless lessons. He now offers the reader, the opportunity to share his learning, as well as how to be strong and enjoy new challenges.

Most of all, there are suggestions on how to achieve turning ideas into successes.

Michelle Obama said: For Barack, success isn't about how much money you make. It's about the difference you make in people's lives.

This could be the author's life mantra.

Irene Harrington OAM JP DGSJ
1988 National President of JCI Australia
JCIA Life Member #4
Past JCIA Senate Chair
National Vice President AFCC (Civil Celebrants)
Awards
JCI Senator
1988 Outstanding National President of the World
2004 Outstanding JCI Senator of the World
2016 Order of Australia Medal (OAM)
2019 Invested as a Dame of Grace (Order of Saint John of Jerusalem)
Life Member of four organisations

About the Author

It might be said that the expression *"Jack of all trades and master of none"* is an apt description of Peter J Snow OAM.

He abandoned pursuit of an engineering degree and accounting qualifications – but his efforts will leave an extraordinary legacy.

He attributes this to the training, skills and self-confidence he gained through membership of JCI (formerly known as Jaycees International) after joining Fremantle Jaycees in 1970.

Obstacles encountered dented (but certainly not overwhelmed) his positive approach and desire to help and mentor others. His vision, entrepreneurial skills and contribution to his community over 70+ years (some of which are referred to in this book) have resulted in a myriad of awards.

International awards for programs developed or overseen by him include: national public relations; awards; fundraising; group collaboration; commercial education; and assistance to the handicapped.

Personal awards include: Voluntary Contribution to Western Australian Heritage; Honorary Tarheel of North Carolina; a Paul Harris fellowship from Rotary; and Community Torchbearer for the Sydney 2000 Olympics.

In addition to being recognised as Outstanding Senator of JCI, Outstanding National Officer and one of the World's Inspiring Jaycees, he was Australian Jaycees (JCIA) first Ambassador in Western Australia and one of the state's Five Outstanding Young Australians.

Along with a JCI Senatorship, he holds life memberships of 8 community or sporting organisations and was awarded an Order of Australia Medal for his contribution to the Australian community. In 2025 he was awarded Life Membership of JCIA.

INTRODUCTION

In *"The New Hustle"* 2017 documentary series it was claimed that 92% of start-ups were doomed to failure. Six years later, the *"Founder"* series on the same subject had this rate at 99%. To put an optimistic spin on these alarming figures, my success rate was well above average - despite the number of projects, that, for many reasons, did not achieve the desired outcomes.

Readers of this book could be forgiven for thinking that many of the stories are works of fiction - given that some of them seem to be so extraordinary that they could not possibly be true. Well, you can be assured that, apart from an embellishment or the odd omission that the passing of time has dimmed from a fading memory, they are, to the greatest extent, factually true.

In some cases, names have been changed, not to protect the innocent, but to avoid unwanted litigation defending the truth of some of the claims made. However, I stand by all of them and, having resolved to die penniless, any person feeling aggrieved by any of my statements is welcome to pursue what will be a dry argument and enriching only their lawyer.

All the projects were learning experiences (some good, some not so good) that have tested focus and resilience from which you may benefit. Many involve fate and luck (both good and bad) – but many also involve timing – hence the sub-title of this book: *"Timing is Everything".* I hope you enjoy the stories.

TIPS FIRST – THEN THE TRUE EXAMPLES THAT CREATED THEM

While always focussed on the goal of whatever I am doing at the time, I am generally impatient with the process of getting to the end result.

For that reason, unlike most books of this type that list lessons learned and tips at the very end, my contrary approach is to list them up front. In that way, the examples that follow will demonstrate how I came to adopt them as my career in venture capital and unusual projects progressed.

In reality, most are just plain common sense - gained from more than half a century at the commercial and not-for-profit organisation coal face!

I do hope you enjoy reading about some of the adventures as much as I did from being involved in them.

If you learn something from them, I will have achieved my aim.

Peter J Snow OAM

Contents

Dedication	3
Foreword	4
About the Author	6
Introduction	7
21 Tips from hard learned Lessons	8, 11
My Entrepreneurial Streak	**13**
Bostock Enterprises	13
Career Decisions?	14
A Taste of Marketing	16
The Wellington Boot	18
A Pearl from Misfortune	19
Exploiting Limitations	20
Back to "real" Work	21
Finding Purpose	22
Controlling my own Destiny	**25**
Naïvety and misplaced trust	
The looming Tempest	**29**
Consequences of absent due diligence	
A Diamond in the Rough	**35**
The deal of a lifetime	
That's not a House – that's a Palace	**41**
Proving the impossible is possible	
Thanks, but NO Thanks – a smart Decision	**47**
Sixth sense decision-making	
CIA – Not the one at Langley, Virginia	**49**
Pioneering with partners	
It was no Joke(r) – Computer Game Pioneers	**53**
Some things are beyond your control	
Revolution assisting Evolution	**66**
Impacting thousands	

CONTENTS (CONTINUED)

A Capital(iser) Idea 69
    Life-changing impact
Solid Foundations and a Vital Investment 73
    Giving back to community
One Man's Journey 76
    Ask and ye shall receive
Venturing Forward 79
    Sharing new ideas
Travel Vision – a Vision too Far ... ahead 81
    What could have been
On the Hoof – Literally! 88
    Recognising defeat
Organically Bad 90
    Second chance misjudgment
Little Friends 97
    Lessons in controlling the supply chain
A Golden Opportunity 101
    Optimising gifts
Where there's a Will ... there's a Way 106
    Solution substitution
It turned into a STAMPede 108
    Changing course to survive
Right Place – Right Time 118
    The stars aligned
From "Rent-a-Cow" to a World Food solution 124
    Understanding Genetics - or lack thereof
A Whale of a Tale! 131
    Optimising opportunism

More by the Author 154

21 TIPS FROM HARD LEARNED LESSONS

1. Have an exit plan/strategy and potential timeline in mind before you start a project or purchase a business. That way, you have a clear goal to aim for. Review periodically.

2. Second chances are fine for potential partners or joint-venturers that have failed or who have had "issues" in the past – but doubly check their background. If any history of dishonesty or unfair dealing is uncovered – graciously decline the proposal and move on. That will almost certainly save you grief in the long term.

3. Always approach a deal on the basis that the worst could happen. Have solutions that minimise risk, cost and loss.

4. Never enter into a 50/50 deal unless you have clear and unambiguous terms to dissolve the arrangement in a way that will avoid costly litigation.

5. Don't be afraid to pioneer - but learn from the experience of others who may have trodden a similar path before and failed. And if you fail, you will have learnt something.

6. Plagiarism and being second to market is fine – just be or do it better!

7. Always leave a deal where both parties feel that they could have done a little better. Don't try and extract the last cent - leave a little something for the next person.

8. Don't worship money, it is a facilitator, not a god.

9. A good team is probably more effective and efficient than doing everything yourself – even if you know you could have done it better.

10. Surround yourself with the best people and set their remuneration (pay and/or share of outcome) accordingly. Look after them. You will get what you paid for.

11. Make sure that your team does not have all "yes" people – welcome at least one "naysayer" who can offer a constructive alternative view and addresses risk.

12. Review all the facts and make a considered decision. The odd mistake you make will be compensated for by the time you saved in not procrastinating through indecision.

13. Always be honest with your partners/stakeholders and they will generally support you in times of difficulty or adversity. If not, you have the wrong partners.

14. Don't sweat the small things – but document things properly – you may need to rely on it later.

15. Give consideration to the worst-case scenario – have a back-up plan that contemplates your absence if it were to occur tomorrow.

16. Always do everything to the best of your ability.

17. Enjoy what you do – or find something that you do enjoy - whether in business or recreation. Life is too short!

18. Do things that will improve your skill set or knowledge.

19. Devote time to making the world a better place personally or in a group/club. You never know where it will lead or who you will meet that may change your life.

20. Be generous with your time when advice is sought.

21. The harder you work, the luckier you will become.

My Entrepreneurial Streak

My primary school education was unremarkable - but my entrepreneurial streak was emerging.

At the age of nine, my mother was embarrassed to receive a phone call about a hand-written sign on a cotton sheet tied to the back of her Morris Minor. It was promoting the sale of the pet rabbits I was breeding.

Bostock Enterprises

By 12, I had imported a small 8" x 5" Adana hand-platen printing press from England and established a small printing business producing tickets for school events, greeting and business cards trading under the name of *Bostock Enterprises*.

A really imaginative name – we lived in Bostock Road.

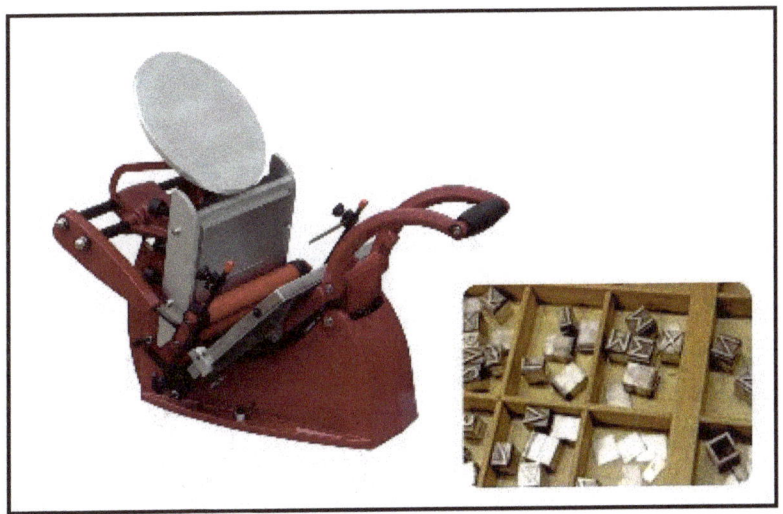

Surprisingly, that little printing machine manufacturer is still in business today. Even refurbished versions of my Adana letterpress printing machine can be purchased for $2,530.

Wish I had kept mine – a 4,260% return is not to be sniffed at – even though it would be over seven decades.

At a Christ Church Grammar School Speech Night, the Headmaster even acknowledged my entrepreneurial flair that had resulted in the significant profit made by the school's "Tuck Shop" under my management.

Watch fob chains bought from Woolworths and re-sold at an appropriate mark-up had created a new fad - and treats like Snow's home-made peanut brickle (no, not brittle) had boosted the result.

CAREER DECISIONS

I was a smart but lazy student and could have done better had I applied myself. Somehow, I managed to get a Commonwealth Scholarship to go to University – it was a given that Snow offspring should go to University and follow in both parents' footsteps.

But at 17, I had no idea what I wanted to do - or be.

Being good at maths and technical drawing, Father said *"Civil Engineering for you"* and I suspect that through his Public Service contacts he may have had a hand in my gaining a Public Works Department Cadetship.

This meant that all fees and books were covered. I would also receive a princely allowance of $4 per week in return for which I was to be locked-in to government employment for a number of years after graduation.

Much to Father's ire and disappointment, after two semesters, I decided that bridge and road building was not my chosen career path. I quit University ... and had to repay the $100 in allowances I had received over my short stint of tertiary education.

[PS: In retrospect, I regretted not just changing courses at the time to something more befitting my natural leanings – and waited another 40 years to return to academia. This time it was to seek a Master of Marketing degree online and then possibly a Doctorate. The irony of two Dr. Snows in the family did have some appeal. However, after being asked if my marketing plan assignment for Australia's last whaling station could be used as course material, I questioned why on earth I was paying for the privilege of learning if my material was better than theirs. With memory also becoming patchy, I abandoned the pursuit of the elusive title, post nominals and wall hanging. But I did at least come away with an Executive Certificate in Marketing - at age 60.]

And so, accounting at night school supplemented a mail-order Hemingway Robertson course in bookkeeping, accountancy and business law basics followed (think of it as distance education in the dark ages). This led to a job as costing clerk and assistant accountant for a small printing company – The Colortype Press.

Although low-profile, it had a few significant clients like the Royal Automobile Club, Swan Brewery Company and Commonwealth Bank and this experience was to greatly benefit me later in life in many projects I became involved in.

With every inch of the factory costed, the company accountant Bill Koek, taught me the intricacies of job costing, pricing methodologies, budgeting and attention to overheads recovery.

LESSON: LISTEN AND LEARN - YOU HAVE TWO EARS AND ONE MOUTH – USE THEM IN THAT PROPORTION.

A Taste of Marketing

My non-work life saw me take on the role as manager of a band – *The Whirlwinds* – a bunch of good blokes – with my best mate Kim Hinton as our "roadie".

It was an exciting achievement getting the group onto Club 17 (Channel 7's equivalent of Rage). Well before the Milli Vanilli lip-syncing scandal, Club 17 used to record sound and then a week later record vision (in which the band mimed to the pre-recorded sound) for later telecast.

In our case, lead singer Alex's commitment to army reserve duties delayed the second session by a month.

This allowed me to negotiate (and underwrite) a recording contract with EMI's HMV label so that the TV host could introduce the group with *"performing their latest single in the shops on Monday...".* It was not a No. 1 hit, but buying all the residual stock at cost allowed them to be autographed and sold for a profit. This particularly applied to country gigs where performances were promoted through a free copy sent to the local radio station.

The ultimate jackpot was exclusive rights to perform at Rottnest Tearooms under a revenue sharing deal with the owner – a hard-as-nails woman you would prefer not to arm-wrestle.

It was the resort island's only suitable venue and "the" place to be on long weekends. That was the case for quite some time until the media exposed the island as a scene of debauchery and under-age (then 21) drinking. The golden goose had finally been plucked when parents banned their teenagers from travelling to this sinful place. Ironically, nothing has really changed in the 50 years since - just relocated to other places as a "Leavers" event.

There was no expense spared on our accommodation but in the middle of summer - not so great. Seven to the room, we were billeted in the workers' quarters - corrugated iron walls and roof, wooden floor, mattresses (straw or possibly Kapok-filled). The wardrobe was a piece of wire from one wall to the other upon which to hang clothes. They were great times!

THE WELLINGTON BOOT

With Kim and members of the band, we opened our own two-level night club in Perth.

Working by day and fitting-out and operating the club after dark stretched human endurance too far. After dropping the lead singer off in Ashfield one 3.00 am, I fell asleep at the wheel and wrote off my Mother's Hillman Imp.

And before you jump to erroneous conclusions - no alcohol was involved. It was a week after my 21st birthday and the opening of our Wellington Boot pleasure palace. It was just exhaustion.

I was later to learn how lucky I was that my femoral artery was not punctured by the broken bones in my leg as paramedics carefully extracted me from the wreckage.

A charge for negligent driving and a bill for the destroyed light pole added insult to injury. Both were later withdrawn out of sympathy for my predicament – at least I was lucky to be alive! The inserted steel shaft proved unsuccessful and bone grafts and eight months on crutches and frequent physiotherapy followed.

A PEARL FROM MISFORTUNE

It was during my recovery that I had my greatest piece of luck – or was it fate? My best mate Kim (who was to become our best man) introduced me to Leona Seghers – his former blind date.

Fortunately, he was keener on her flatmate, Sue. So, after my first post-recovery Saturday afternoon outing for a few drinks with Kim, we went around to a flat in Kings Park Road, West Perth, where I met Leona - with hair in curlers and the worst cup of coffee I have ever endured. Fair to say it wasn't love at first sight, but I was on crutches and couldn't escape (that's my story) – but love developed from there. More than two life sentences and we are still together – and for that I am eternally grateful.

This was also the time of the Vietnam War when birthdates of 20-year-olds were randomly selected to decide who would become conscripted as soldiers. Unusually lucky at raffles, it was no surprise that April 10 was a winning conscription marble - but also, being on crutches with a steel pin in my leg, I failed the army's medical.

I was indeed lucky not to go where many young Australians would die in a futile conflict. Luck would follow me through life.

Timing is Everything | Peter J Snow OAM

EXPLOITING LIMITATIONS

The leg injury also ended my rugby career after representing the state in two Under 21 games. But heeding advice to avoid contact sport, giving up the game I really enjoyed allowed me to establish *Western Entertainment Service* – a band booking agency that I could run from home handling up to 40 of Perth's bands.

This led to an invitation to develop and run *Spectrum* nightclub on behalf of some well-heeled locals who liked the idea of owning Perth's first suburban BYO nightclub. It was on the first floor of Claremont Shopping Centre - next to what is now the Claremont Hotel.

Exciting times - bringing top Australian groups to Perth with my imposing best mate as dinner-suited doorman/bouncer.   Opening night with Marty Rhone had 400 inside and many hundreds pushing against the full height plate glass walls to gain entrance. Police had to be called to control the crowd and later acts including John Farnham, Masters Apprentices, The Groop and many more, drew crowds.

Without liquor sales, revenue was only from entry fees and food and non-alcoholic beverage sales - so viability depended on the quality of the acts presented. After eight months, the novelty had worn off for the owners and, reluctant to spend more to refresh the very basic venue or continue to fund top talent, they sold out.

Spectrum became the *Crazy Elephant*. The new owner only lasted three months.

LESSON:
CONSIDER A PROPOSED BUSINESS ACTIVITY AGAINST INDUSTRY TRENDS AND BUDGET BOTH FUTURE & FINANCES ACCORDINGLY.

BACK TO "REAL" WORK

It was time for a real job.

I was lucky (without formal qualifications) to get a job as Accountant for the Tel Vu Group of companies. That comprised four retail electrical goods stores, a TV rental and service company, finance company and had WA's sole Clark Rubber franchise.

After re-oganising and streamlining of the accounting and administrative functions, I became concerned about the integrity of the managing director and started to look elsewhere.

A very flattering reference from the partner of the external accountants saw me land a job as accountant for a fast-growing Mayday Hire Service run by Warren Jones and Peter Anderson.

Warren was the most dynamic and motivational person I have ever met. He went on to be the real brains behind Australia II's famous win of the 1983 America's Cup for which Alan Bond claimed the glory.

Although more than half a century ago, Warren's advice is still firmly in my mind:

LESSON:
"CONSIDER ALL THE FACTS IN A SITUATION AND MAKE A DECISION. WE WILL ACCEPT THE ODD MISTAKE THAT MAY RESULT - BUT THIS WILL BE MORE THAN OFFSET BY THE TIME YOU SAVE BY NOT PROCRASTINATING ADDED TO THE EXTRA PRODUCTIVITY THROUGH GETTING ON WITH OTHER THINGS".

FINDING PURPOSE

Mayday had a very wise policy of paying the fees of any service club staff wished to join and this was to change my life.

Warren, along with high profile car dealer John Hughes and the ultimately infamous Alan Bond, had all been members of Fremantle Jaycees – part of the world-wide young people's personal development organisation known as Junior Chamber International – and having ignored marketing gurus' basic advice about avoiding acronyms – is now known as JCI.

Established in 1934, Fremantle was Australia's second oldest Jaycee chapter. Ironically, a rugby mate Phil Barton took me along as a guest to Warren's old club.

What particularly appealed to me was the training in public speaking.

As with the majority of people, I had a fear of speaking in other than a one-to-one situation.

That training enabled me to address audiences of many thousands at Jaycees World Congresses and as a guest speaker on many other occasions.

Within 12 months of joining in 1970, my focus had changed from personal self-interest to projects that could benefit the community - but it also developed within me a greater self-confidence.

LESSON: ENCOURAGE STAFF TO JOIN A COMMUNITY GROUP

In the early 1970's, Mayday (which also had equipment manufacturing and sales divisions) had other branches including one in Darwin which was subsequently destroyed by Cyclone Tracy.

Expansion had been partly funded by a placement of one third of the equity to Amalgamated Industries Ltd - a division of Alan Bond's Bond Corporation.

Bond then used an "Explosion Clause" in the Shareholder Agreement to acquire the remaining 66% of the shares.

For those bringing in third party investment, this is a clever clause that works on the basis that either party may make an offer for the other's shares at any time. If declined, then the offeree is obliged to buy the offeror's shares at the same rate per share – much like a put option. That generally sets a fair value on the business and assumes that the offeree can (if necessary) borrow the funds to buy out the offeror.

In this case, it became apparent that although Bond did seek the successful business, he was really after Warren to head up his growing industrial conglomerate.

Amalgamated Industries Ltd included hardware, glass, a bowling alley, land/property development and now, equipment hire, manufacturing and sales.

Accounting administration was to be consolidated at a new head office currently under construction and I would become just one accountant among many.

Aware of my marketing flair, Warren offered me a different position to the very mundane accounting position at the head office – as Sales Administration Manager of Skipper Mayday Machinery Ltd.

I had responsibility for merging accounting and administrative functions of Warren's high-flying, service-driven hire business with a 60-year-old machinery supply and service company where the request for a new pencil required a return of the stub of the old one to the General Manager.

Integrating and streamlining service-at-any-cost with a rigid process-driven system was an interesting and fulfilling challenge.

LESSONS:
1. PERIODICALLY REVIEW ADMINISTRATIVE SYSTEMS - ARE THEY ARE STILL ESSENTIAL OR JUST MAINTAINED BECAUSE IT HAS ALWAYS BEEN DONE THAT WAY?
2. CONSIDER BOTS AND THE USE OF AI TO ELIMINATE MANUAL LABOUR.
3. USE AN "EXPLOSION CLAUSE" IN EQUITY AGREEMENTS.

CONTROLLING MY OWN DESTINY – A MA(HER)D IDEA

Always on the look-out for new business ideas, in early 1973 I answered a newspaper advertisement in the Public Notices column. It sought Investor/Directors for a new form of housing finance business.

For $5,000, Queensland-based promoters led by a Brian Maher were offering three WA investors 20% each of a new company - modelled on their existing Queensland and New South Wales operations.

Recognising a potentially big market for cheap home loans - but lacking 60% of the required funds, I sold the idea to five friends - two of whom were colleagues at Mayday Hire - which is an important introduction to later stories.

The five collectively contributed the remaining $3,000 for a half interest but at a small premium and so I formed *Management Consortiums Pty Ltd* to hold our 20% investment in the new venture.

With funding in place and Jaycees-developed self-confidence, I thanked Warren for the opportunities he had given me and embraced the risk of self-employment.

As Executive Director of the fledgling Federated Mutual Home Loans Fund (WA) Ltd and its related management company, I was to work with Managing Director Bill Tolhurst, a retired Westpac (then known as the Bank of NSW) Manager.

Eight months later and with 60% of the initial $25,000 capital gone, lawyers discovered that WA's unique building society laws prohibited our plan.

So much for risk analysis and local research and, as it turned out, misplaced trust and lack of investigation into the background of the proponents who had offered us what appeared to be a great idea.

However, Maher came up with a way to recoup our losses and move on.

It involved buying companies with taxable income.

The Queenslanders had a "black box" to deal with the taxable income and neutralise the current year tax problem so that they could pay an apparent "premium" to acquire "profit-pregnant" companies. Being both young and naïve, I accepted Maher's representations that he had legal advice on the effectiveness of his income neutralisation process.

His rebuttal of our enquiries was on his oft-stated position *"that he was not in the business of spawning competitors"*.

To me this was simply accepted as comparable with Coca Cola's protection of its intellectual property.

The vendors would be better off because, at that point, profit from sales of shares in private companies held for more than 12 months was a tax-free capital gain - based on the legal precedent of the Slutzkin court case.

At one point Maher said to me: *"Stick with me kid, and I'll make you rich."* And he did, but that should have set off warning bells.

Bill and I implemented the new strategy reliant on trust and good faith which, with the benefit of hindsight, should have been tempered by due diligence.

Naïve we indeed were - as were our counterparts in NSW and Victoria and a new local "partner" Ron Woss - who replaced Bill when he retired. I learnt a lot from working with Ron - about the way I did not want to conduct my business dealings with people in the future.

This was an era where tax avoidance (not evasion) was almost considered a national sport and not taboo as it is today.

Early in our new direction, Rod Todman, an astute investigator from the Perth Tax Office, called at our office as the first stage of an enquiry. I happily provided him with access to all the records for the 17 companies I had acquired thus far for the Maher group.

Never hearing from Todman again reaffirmed my belief that whatever process Maher was applying to neutralise the taxable income must indeed be effective.

Over the next four years I co-ordinated the acquisition of up to 300 companies and many of the Perth establishment were my clients. Confidentiality and attention to detail were key pillars of the business.

My settlements amounted to millions of dollars.

After nearly five years, Maher must have had an inkling that the end was nigh, as in about 1978, we were advised that the business was to be wound down nationally.

My original backers and I opted to sell our investment vehicle *Management Consortiums Pty Ltd* as part of that wind-down process. They received a "capital" profit of about nine times their original investment. We were all happy with that return.

Ultimately, Bill and I never saw our share of a "contingency" fund that we had contributed to for a "rainy day", but by way of compensation for closing down, Bill and I received a "bonus" in the form of Mt. Augustus Station. Its real claim to fame is that it boasts the world's largest monolithic rocky outcrop - about twice the size of the more famous Uluru.

We were quick to sell it to the station manager's family as we had no desire to become landed gentry on almost one million acres of pastoral lease that had just survived two years of drought.

It had been one of the group's first asset-backed acquisitions way back in about 1975. At sale, it only had about 1,500 head of cattle.

Timing is Everything | Peter J Snow OAM

THE LOOMING TEMPEST

As we were to find out much later, Maher's "black box" had been a myth – Maher and his Queensland cohorts just pillaged the companies' funds.

They then transferred ownership to some unsuspecting soul associated with the Painters and Dockers Union attracted by the offer of weekend on the Gold Coast and a thousand dollars in cash. In return they just signed a large volume of consents to act as a Director and Secretary of all the companies acquired across Australia and share transfers in the main acquiring company.

Apparently, Todman's files that I had willingly provided to him had supported a QC's recommendation that criminal charges be laid. But they weren't – until many years later.

There is a certain irony about the bureaucracy's mishandling of the whole affair at great cost to the Australian taxpayer. It was estimated that the lost revenue from about 6,000 companies involved across Australia in this scandal was up to $1 billion.

It is horrifying to think that the whole scheme could have (and should have) been nipped in the bud had Todman's report been properly dealt with. Did anyone lose their job over this debacle? No, well yes, one did but for another reason.

Five years of delays within the Crown Solicitor's Office saw the Australian Tax Office advised that the case was to be abandoned for insufficient evidence.

The matter only came to light in 1982 when the Costigan Royal Commission into a Union uncovered bank transactions involving millions of dollars.

The paper trail ultimately led to a bottom drawer in the Crown Solicitor's Perth Office.

It was only then then that the proverbial hit the fan.

Little did we know that the Costigan Royal Commission would become known for the *"Bottom of the Harbour"* scheme - the basis of Australia's biggest corporate fraud of the 1970's and criminal conspiracy charges for defrauding the Commonwealth for Maher and all his associates across Australia.

And that included Bill Tolhurst, Ron Woss and me.

Timing is Everything | Peter J Snow OAM

The media had a field-day, and I quickly came to appreciate (not!) the term *"trial by media"*. Australia's first retrospective tax legislation was also introduced and joint and several "Promoter's Tax" saw me with a huge personal tax liability – many multiples of any benefits I had actually received from the Maher Group.

Along with other vendors, additional retrospective legislation resulted in tax assessments and penalties to those who had anticipated their proceeds of sale would be tax-free capital gains.

In our case, this proved to be a relationship breaker for three of my five original "backers".

Having sold their shares at 10 times their original investment in the late 1970's, and long since spent the windfall, they were now confronted with assessments and penalties equivalent to about 60% of their "profit".

Disappointingly, they blamed me for the retrospective legislation that had put them in that predicament.

They chose to ignore the fact that, even after payment of the unwanted tax bills and ignoring various dividends over the years, they had actually received a net 400% return on their original investment.

Strange how some people react to adversity when money is involved.

The conspiracy charges could not have come at a worse time for me. I had just been named as one the Five Outstanding Young Australians in Western Australia. It was gut-wrenching to have to go to my children's schools to warn teachers of the media storm about to erupt over my impending arrest by Federal Police.

Some children can be quite nasty given an opportunity to do so. Fortunately, my warnings to the teachers had been unnecessary.

I spent half a day in the Police lock-up before being bailed by one of my loyal shareholders.

Removal of belt and shoelaces brings home the reality of incarceration.

It would then be two years before a committal hearing. A week into the hearing, one of my co-accused, Bill Tolhurst, suicided. Then in his mid-sixties, with the onset of dementia and refused legal aid, he could not face the ordeal of lengthy committal proceedings.

His death eliminated his charges, but the prosecution denied his request for his dying protestation of innocence to be read into the court transcript.

Bill's widow, Joan, was to offer sage advice that forever sticks in my mind over the public perception of what we had been alleged to have done - but knew we were not guilty of:

"The people who matter don't mind and the people who mind don't matter." Sage advice indeed!

After the shock of criminal charges, my luck was to turn in the form of Magistrate Josh Forrest who claimed to be an industrial magistrate from the bush with no experience in commerce - but said he would get to the bottom of the matter.

Given the millions of dollars involved in the company acquisitions and the Magistrate's lack of commercial experience, my immediate reaction was we would be wrongly convicted.

Timing is Everything | Peter J Snow OAM

But true to his word, after a 56-day hearing and 42 witnesses, Magistrate Forrest said that all the evidence, including my attention to documentation, lodgement of corporate affairs and taxation documents and airfreighting of records to head office in Queensland defied suggestions of any fraudulent intent.

It was clear to him that we were unaware of the true destination of the companies we had acquired through the Perth office.

Ron and I were discharged with *"no case to answer"*.

Unfortunately, Bill Tolhurst was not with us to celebrate.

The media space devoted to the dismissal of the case was a mere fraction of the extensive coverage leading up to the charges and the hearing.

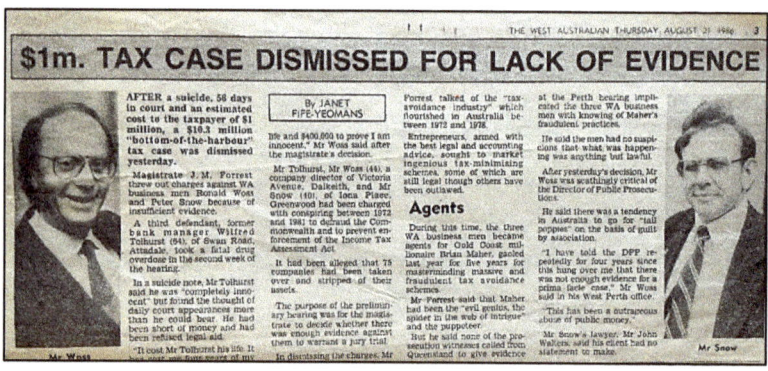

As you can imagine, this lengthy period was traumatic for the whole family and left my usual optimism and self-esteem badly dented. It took several years to recover - but Leona was my rock throughout the ordeal.

Timing is Everything | Peter J Snow OAM

A Diamond in the Rough

But brighter things were to come.

In the late 1970's the two Mayday Hire colleagues who had partially bankrolled my investment in Federated, asked me to buy them out.

I was puzzled by the request as their shares in Management Consortiums were increasing in value and yielding a handsome annual return.

On questioning their reasons, they expressed a desire to start their own equipment hire business.

I declined their request but offered to join them on the basis that my knowledge of the accounting and administration of a hire business from my Mayday days coupled with my corporate experience, would be of benefit to them.

Thus, I became a one-third owner and silent partner in *Diamond Hire* with responsibility for setting up the family trusts and operating unit trust as well as facilitating the funding for the first hire branch building in Wanneroo Road, Greenwood.

In quick time the business grew to the point where a second branch was opened in Albany Highway, Cannington.

Some 18 months later, Wreckair came knocking.

This publicly-listed hire company wanted to move into Western Australia and saw Diamond Hire as the opportunity to do so.

Although Cannington was not yet making a profit, a generally acceptable deal was agreed and prompt finalisation promised.

As the months dragged on, when pressed about the delays, Wreckair's Managing Director, Ray Kelsey, confided that while his Australian Board had signed off on the deal there was a problem. Wreckair's major shareholder was American-based Consolidated Pneumatic Holdings. It was the time of the Iranian hostage crisis, and the major shareholder had vetoed expansion moves by any companies it controlled pending resolution of the conflict. And so, the potential sale of Diamond Hire became a casualty of events in the middle east.

Given the promise of a quick deal, we were less than happy - but parted ways amicably - understanding that the decision was beyond Ray and his Board's control.

So, what or where to next? It came to our attention that a compatible business called *Stateside Hire* was a potential acquisition. It hired site sheds and toilets, brick hoists and scaffolding and would complement Diamond's range of general builders and handyman equipment.

The back story was unique, the investor-owner, David Sheppard, had fallen out with the manager, a family member, and replaced him with his in-house accountant, Gary Bettridge.

It had been intended to be a short-term arrangement but after four years, Accountant Bettridge wanted to move on - and owner Sheppard did not fancy a hands-on role.

Timing is Everything | Peter J Snow OAM

It seemed like an ideal marriage – and proved to be.

Stateside was twice the size of Diamond Hire in turnover and personnel and with both parties willing, a deal was struck.

Financing was a problem.

Our bank would not fund second-hand equipment nor do a lease-back deal on the Balcatta premises.

In the absence of alternatives, Sheppard agreed to retain and lease us the premises and assign to us 11 equipment financing agreements. He also agreed to carry terms on the purchase price - with payment to be made over five years. A very willing seller.

Eight months later, while we were still digesting an acquisition that had trebled our staff to 39 and hire revenue to $2 million, I was flying from Hobart to Melbourne when an Australian Financial Review headline hit my eye: *"Repco buys Wreckair".*

Immediately on landing in Melbourne, I called Wreckair's Managing Director and commenced the discussion with:
"Congratulations on your new owner. We are three times the size and the price has gone up!"

Ray admitted that he had been to Western Australia a few times since the previous collapsed sale negotiations but had been too embarrassed to make contact.

He confirmed that they were still extremely interested and undertook to get back to us quickly.

As a precursor to further discussions, I reviewed media coverage of Repco's acquisition of Wreckair and also came across the following article from an edition of hire industry journal Hire & Rental Australasia:

REPCO BUYS WRECKAIR

Repco Ltd., a leading Automative parts and engineering group has made a $23 million bid for Wreckair Holdings, one of Australias largest equipment hire groups.

Major shareholder, the U.S. group Consolidated P eumatic Holdings Ltd., received $7.19 per share or approx. $15 million for its 65 percent shareholding in Wreckair which it acquired for $3.60 per share in 1972.

Mr. Neil Walford, Repco Chairman said Wreckair had an impressive growth record and had very good future growth prospects. Repco would be able to provide the financial support to ensure Wreckair a high rate of growth.

Wreckairs 1980 profit, just released, indicated a strong second half recovery for the group after the financial strain of opening five new depots, which forced first half profits down 32 percent despite a 21 percent rise in revenue.

Profit for the fun year was down only 3 percent from $1.82 million to $1.7 million. Revenue for the 12 months was up 25 percent to $25 million. Wreckairs profit in the December half was up 22 percent from $983,000 to $1.2 million, Reflecting some improvement in the building and construction market late in the year.

On close analysis, I was mystified at the share price paid for the takeover. Repco appeared to have paid far too much.

This prompted me to call Wreckair's Chief Financial Officer, Peter Penman to determine whether there were any off-balance sheet assets that had inflated the price to 10 times earnings when the market at the time was a fraction of that multiple.

The answer was "no", but when pressed, he divulged that it was the price Consolidated was prepared to accept for its shares.

Armed with that invaluable knowledge, I did some profitability projections and calculations as to our potential sale price - no price having been discussed with Wreckair at this point.

Consultation with the senior tax partner and other advisors at Price Waterhouse confirmed the efficacy of my calculations and I then met with my two "operating" partners in the business.

As part of the deal would involve them in five-year contracts to stay with the business, they had to be happy with any proposed deal – if not, there would be no deal.

I approached it this way:

"Remembering you will be locked in for five years, how much will you accept in your pocket for your one third of the business?"

After some deliberation, both nominated roughly the same figure. When I said: *"I think I can get us 50% more than that"*, I was astounded when one replied that he wouldn't accept a cent less than the figure I had nominated – 10 times "projected earnings" for the forthcoming year.

It left me with no wriggle room in negotiations but that was the price we nominated, and it was accepted by Wreckair without debate.

Maybe we should have asked for more?

Maybe not!

It was a very good deal by any standard !

A month later, with my two partners in Melbourne to meet Wreckair's other state managers, I called and asked for the return of the sale documents so that I could arrange transfer duty stamping and registration.

I was astounded to learn that the documents had yet to be signed, yet the full payment for the sale of the business was already in our bank account.

So much for corporate governance!

As Kerry Packer was alleged to have said of his sale of the Nine Network to Alan Bond and buy back at a quarter of the sale price:

"You only get one Alan Bond in your lifetime".

LESSON:
"YOU ONLY GET ONE WRECKAIR IN YOUR LIFETIME".

There was an additional sweetener in the deal.
We were able to secure a nice discount by paying out the vendor of Stateside Hire four years earlier than he (or we) had expected.

LESSONS:
1. TIMING IS EVERYTHING!
2. IN ANY SALE, UNDERSTAND YOU BUYER'S MOTIVATION AND BENCHMARK (IF YOU CAN DETERMINE IT) THEN PITCH WITH FLEXIBILITY IN MIND.

THAT'S NOT A HOUSE – THAT'S A PALACE!

Having had to borrow 90% of the $10,500 purchase price for our first home in Kewdale, the Wreckair sale allowed us to "invest" in a "forever palace" in Greenwood.

Mistake One: It should have been built in the adjoining suburb.

We acquired three blocks, one for the house, one for a potential tennis court and one overlooking our back yard (so that we could protect our privacy by controlling what was built on it).

My brother-in-law from New South Wales was its top apprentice bricklayer. John Seghers also had a Building Licence and agreed to come over and build our dream home. He did a great job.

We had it designed by an architect – a father we had met at the kids' tee-ball. One does these things when young, foolish, flush with funds and not thinking long-term.

Mistake Two: No expense spared – it would have everything.

With me frequently travelling, the 80,000-brick construction took nearly 18-months due to decisions on issues deferred pending my return.

Three split levels, fully ducted air-conditioning, sauna, spa, pool and a two-room office suite with its own entrance, telephone and intercom system.

The perfect home office arrangement.

The dream was shattered when an unresolved teacher-child issue at the local primary school required us to move our two children into private schools in Claremont.

In doing so, we had not considered transport issues. At the time, there was no convenient bus connection. That meant a 20-minute car shuttle twice a day to the Karrinyup bus terminal. And, more often than not, extra trips to Claremont before or after sports' training.

The novelty quickly wore off and we rented closer to the schools on a direct bus route.

So much for the "forever" home on which no expense had been spared.

The question arose as how we could optimise the sale of a property on which we had overcapitalised by at least 50% more than any property in the surrounding area.

Consulting Bill Goddard of Goddard & Goddard, an auctioneer friend through Jaycees, I was advised that we would be battling to get anywhere near our money back.

That constituted a challenge for me to prove him wrong. On learning that about 80% of properties are sold through local real estate agents or friends who have friends wanting to move to the area,

I came up with a strategy. It was based on his suggestion that an auction may identify a buyer prepared to pay for a very unique property – which ours certainly was – but no guarantee.

Timing is Everything | Peter J Snow OAM

I spared no expense in producing a 6-page full-colour laminated brochure – even having the photographer take early evening photos of the pool and other features.

The only things missing were the address and a price.

Timing is Everything | Peter J Snow OAM

Formal Entertaining Area

The main entrance lobby leads to an intimate setting which comfortably seats 10 for a moodlit dinner and then one step up to an extravagant lounge and cocktails area featuring exposed beams and lush Regal Berber quality carpeting opening on to a tiled outdoor viewing balcony.

The warmth of friendly conversation is encouraged by the feature-brick fireplace complete with built-in curtain mesh firescreen and grate trapdoor chute which enables the ash to find its way to a sealed bin in the garage below.

As might be expected, not only this area, but all parts of this tastefully decorated luxury home feature quality window treatments and exquisite light fittings as well as the best floorcoverings.

Library/Music Room

This thoughtful inclusion provides the budding musician or student with a special quiet room away from the living area complete with built-in desk and extensive bookshelves.

Fully Ducted Reverse-cycle Airconditioning

Two separate reverse-cycle airconditioners provide fully ducted comfort to the four living zones.

The formal entertaining area, games room, 4 bedrooms and kitchen, family and meals area can each have their own thermostat creating the ultimate in comfort during cold winter nights and hot summer days.

Outdoor Entertaining

The aroma of steak and sausages cooking on the five-burner mains-connected gas barbeque attracts guests to the pergola-covered entertaining area near the pool, spa and sauna.

Decked with permanently fitted party lights this area is but four steps to the adjoining block which has landscaped native gardens and an extensive lawn area suitable for the tennis enthusiast. It's even been used for the odd game of cricket.

Fully Reticulated Landscaped Lawns and Gardens

A 12-station 2-cycle fully automatic reticulation system keeps the landscaped lawns and gardens precision watered in the quiet of the early morning.

Twenty copies of the fancy brochure were given to every local real estate agent with the advice that the incentive of a 50% bonus on the going commission rate would apply subject to them:

1. NOT disclosing the address of the property.

2. Bringing a potential buyer (without revealing the address) for a private inspection on 24-hour's notice AFTER they have fallen in love with what they have seen in the brochure.

   [This would allow us to set up wafting smells of freshly brewed coffee or bread baking in a bread maker]

3. NOT indicating or discussing price - as we would entertain offers and negotiate on their offer but would not nominate a price range.

Surprisingly, a young couple from Carine (where, with the benefit of hindsight we should have built) had a growing family.

They liked what they saw in the brochure and put in an offer close to what we had hoped. After a little haggling and, despite the prospective buyer's wife's nervousness about the size of the mortgage they would need, a deal was done a week before the scheduled auction date.

To Bill Goddard's surprise, the sale did recoup our cost and Bill admitted, after years in business, he had learnt a new way to sell.

POSTSCRIPT: A few months after the sale, the buyer asked me to call by and open the wall safe in the office suite on the ground floor. He had forgotten the instructions and codes.

After demonstrating the unlocking procedure to him, he reminded me of his wife's mortgage nervousness.

With a cheeky but sheepish grin, he showed me a photocopy of a cheque from Lotterywest dated a month or so earlier.

The amount was close to the purchase price of the house.

Now that's karma! All parties had a win!

LESSONS:
1. DON'T SPEND LAVISHLY BECAUSE YOU CAN.
2. WHEN YOU SHOOT YOURSELF IN THE FOOT, LOOK FOR THE RIGHT DRESSING TO PATCH THE HOLE.
3. THINK OUTSIDE THE SQUARE AFTER UNDERSTANDING THE TRADITIONAL WAYS OF DOING THINGS.
4. DARE TO BE DIFFERENT.

Thanks, but NO Thanks – A Smart Decision!

With my son's involvement in junior football from the age of five, his fledgling club in the northern suburbs needed resources to fit out its swelling number of teams that now numbered about 30.

I joined the Committee of Northern Districts Junior Football Club, took on the role of sponsorship co-ordinator and went about my task with almost religious fervour. It was when quiz nights were in vogue and our committee was able to assemble a big range of prizes.

The local member of Parliament, former Journalist, Brian Burke, MLA, saw the opportunity for exposure to another group of voters and readily agreed to act as quizmaster. He was an excellent MC and our quiz nights were big successes - raising thousands of dollars – and becoming an annual event.

After Brian escalated up the Labor Party ladder and became the youngest Leader of the State Opposition, the Football Club's President called me with an invitation to see Brian at his Parliament House office.

With no inkling as to what this was about, I duly attended the seat of power and was greeted by an affable Brian with an opening statement: *"I know our politics are diametrically opposed, but let's talk about money."*

My response was: *"Our politics are NOT diametrically opposed Brian as I do NOT have a publicly expressed position on politics."*

Brian then explained that many in his party thought that raising a few hundred dollars via small events was considered fund-raising - but he had bigger ideas.

He planned to tap *"the big end of town"* and, having been impressed by how I operated, wanted me to co-ordinate the whole show. The aim was to solicit much larger amounts of money to support Labor in its election campaigns. He outlined his vision for what was to become the Curtin Foundation.

While impressed with his grandiose big picture idea (which I thought had half a chance) and although the prospect of extending my network had appeal, a sixth sense triggered my response: *"I am very flattered, but my plans do not include raising money for the Labor Party or, in fact, any political party - but thank you for the invitation"*, and promptly took my leave.

Brian achieved his aim with the Curtin Foundation, which at one time boasted the cream of the Perth establishment as supporters. Ultimately his dealings with the "big end of town" led to the public furore known as WA Inc. He was alienated from the party he had driven and is banned from contact with Labour Ministers.

Somewhat ironically, several years after his declined invitation, Brian and I were both named as one of Western Australia's Five Outstanding Young Australians at the same 1982 awards ceremony conducted by Australian Jaycees (now JCI Australia).

LESSON:
HEED ANY SIXTH SENSE WARNING OR GUT FEEL.

CIA – NOT THE ONE AT LANGLEY, VIRGINIA

Being an entrepreneurial bunch, members of Fremantle Jaycees took up the idea of forming an investment club.

With a warped sense of humour over the acronym it would be known by, we bought a shell company and renamed it *Corporate Investments of Australia Pty Ltd* (CIA for short). It was a mutual fund of sorts and evolved to have many contributory members.

Each committed to contributing $40 per month as share capital. As the pool of funds grew, all were encouraged to keep an eye out for any potential investment opportunities – aimed more at private equity than listed shares.

With the passage of time, how the first significant venture came to our attention has long been forgotten – but it seemed a great idea at the time – and appeared to be a great opportunity.

CIA became pioneers in new manufacturing technology.

If you have graced a recliner arm-chair with a lever-controlled foot-rest, did you ever wonder why they are so expensive?

The answer is simple – they are assembled from hundreds of parts – in fact, the Jason Laz-y-boy chairs at the time had more than 350 components – making them very labour-intensive and justifiably costly.

On closer scrutiny, even the foam on the foot-rest was individually "shaped" and the shape or size of each piece could vary materially.

This necessitated considerable adjustment when they were upholstered and then glued to the wooden base before being attached to the lever-operated concertina arms.

There was obviously a need for a better way!

Why do you need to know this?

Because it was the basis of CIA's first joint-venture.

Our research included me adding German and Italian production plants to a business trip to Europe before attending my first Jaycees World Congress in Amsterdam.

In the port city of Ancona on Italy's east coast, I saw ornate shaped doors for kitchen cupboards and drawers produced in rigid polyurethane. They only required painting prior to fitting. Once set, each could be cut and drilled into – treated just like wood. Flexible foam could be produced in the same way for the foot piece. There was Jason's answer.

The principle was simple. Inject two chemicals into a fibreglass or alloy mould and it set in the shape of the mould.

Out popped moulded foam – in a consistent size and shape. This was cold-cure moulding at its best and identified a big opportunity to develop a business in two stages. Firstly, in flexible foam for Jason foot and head-rests and then, as a second stage, replace the wood by expanding into rigid polyurethane production.

The long-term idea was that the footrest could be produced as one single consistent sized and shaped piece – soft flexible foam on top and rigid foam underneath – no gluing required.

It was a great concept that appealed to management at Jason.

Structural Mouldings Pty Ltd was formed as a CIA-Jason joint-venture. It was Western Australia's first cold-cure polyurethane foam moulding manufacturer.

The resulting Business Plan was based on Jason's commitment to a minimum annual requirement that showed it would be a viable and profitable business from day one.

Jason's contribution was the allocation of one of its factory buildings fitted out with exhaust fans to extract the noxious fumes produced by the isocyanate chemicals used in the mixing and production process.

CIA provided the operational funding and purchased the machine imported from Germany and flew in an installer who also trained the two staff. Our young shareholder group had immense pride when the Minister for Industrial Development, Andrew Mensaros MLA officially opened the first production plant of its type in Western Australia.

It was an exciting time.

However, as time went on, and the funds were diminishing, it was clear that all was not as it should be.

Jason's orders never exceeded 20% of its commitment upon which the joint-venture had been based.

It was time to bring the matter to a head.

At the final meeting with Jason's Managing Director, Jack Bridge, he conceded that they had not kept to their end of the deal.

Being an honourable pillar of the Uniting Church, he agreed to buy out CIA's 50% of Structural Mouldings Pty Ltd and repay CIA's loan funding thus recouping all of CIA's investment in the project.

Nice to meet really honourable people like Jack in a cut-throat business world!

CIA was now on the look-out for its next foray into the world of private equity.

LESSONS:
1. CONTEMPLATE EXIT STRATEGIES FOR VARIOUS SCENARIOS (BOTH BEST AND WORST CASES) – BUT DO SO BEFORE YOU START.
2. IDEALLY DEAL WITH PEOPLE WHOSE VERBAL AGREEMENT OR HANDSHAKE DEAL IS THEIR BOND – BUT HAVE A STAKEHOLDER AGREEMENT TO RELY ON AS YOUR FALL-BACK POSITION.

Timing is Everything | Peter J Snow OAM

IT WAS NO JOKE(R)

COMPUTER GAME PIONEERS

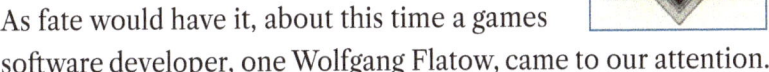

As fate would have it, about this time a games software developer, one Wolfgang Flatow, came to our attention.

His creations in professional packaging looked interesting. In reviewing the games market, it puzzled me why most computer games were only available on one or two computer platforms.

The reason offered by Flatow was that developers traditionally develop a game on their platform of choice.

I asked how many platforms he could develop his primary game "Joker Poker" for.

Six was the answer.

The next question was how do you maximise sales by stopping the creation of pirate copies?

Simple! Just modify the software by linking it to a contest with a significant prize where the computer generates a code unique to that disc, the score and that machine? Each game box could include five (one-a-month) mail-in entry coupons so that players could enter their score and unique code.

The unique code and the absence of mail-in entry coupons would deter pirates. Copied discs would not generate the required code and a second user would not have the specially printed entry coupons.

Even simpler – make the draw for the major prize play-off random rather than tied to highest scores.

Sounded like a good plan ,.. and it was!

What was the biggest market? North America, of course!

With CIA not having the total funds required, we syndicated other investors via a limited partnership, set up a unit trust under *Joker Software International Pty Ltd* as trustee and a joint-venture with Flatow's company Joker Software Games Pty Ltd.

Then, off to America I went with the concept of a US$200,000 contest for 20 North American finalists playing off for a first prize of $100,000 cash.

What was even better, the contest costs constituted export marketing expenditure and $200,000 could be claimed back as a grant under a government export incentive program known as the Export Market Development Grant Scheme.

FOR IMMEDIATE RELEASE

MINDSCAPE INC
3444 DUNDEE ROAD
NORTHBROOK, IL 60062
312/480-7667

MEDIA UPDATE

Contact:
Lisa Petrison (ext. 255)

AUSSIE JOKER POKER INTRODUCTION
TO INCLUDE $200,000 SWEEPSTAKES

NORTHBROOK, IL -- November 10, 1988 -- **Aussie Joker Poker**, a computerized card game popular in Australia, has been released in the United States on all major computer formats.

In **Aussie Joker Poker**, the computer acts as the dealer and croupier, and distributes the winnings at the end of each game. Up to 90 players can compete against one another, and can tailor the deck sizes and rounds per player to suit their preferences.

The game was created by Australian-based Joker Software International and is distributed by Mindscape.

The introduction of **Aussie Joker Poker** will be backed with a sweepstakes featuring $200,000 in cash and prizes. The contest will fly 20 people to Las Vegas to compete in an **Aussie Joker Poker** competition with a top prize of $100,000.

Contest finalists will be chosen at random from persons sending in entry blanks before April 30, 1989. They will receive a round trip for two to Las Vegas and a two-night stay at the Golden Nugget Hotel, as well as a chance to win the top prize or $25,000 in other prizes.

-more-

TELEX: 206699 MINDSCAPE UD   FAX: 312-480-0496

The Golden Nugget Casino in Las Vegas provisionally agreed to host the national playoff by the 20 finalists drawn randomly from all entry coupons received.

Mindscape Inc, whose then Vice President was an Australian, was keen to be our distributor – especially when it was revealed that there were three other products to follow.

At a Computer Games Expo on the east coast, I conducted a survey of journalists from all relevant computer magazines specialising in the six intended platforms. The was to estimate minimum sales based on the product, the contest, advertising campaign and in-store promotion.

The answers were very encouraging and ranged from 110,000 to 180,000 units.

Considering our breakeven was 42,000 units and our distributor Mindscape had agreed to an initial order of 22,000 units with healthy margins– we looked to be on a real winner! And we had an additional level of comfort in dealing with a fellow Aussie at a leading global computer games distributor.

Timing is Everything | Peter J Snow OAM

Timing is Everything | Peter J Snow OAM

☑ **AUSTRALIAN OFFICE:**
Suite 7, Abacus House, 30 Angove Street,
North Perth, WESTERN AUSTRALIA 6006
Correspondence to: P.O. Box 308,
West Perth, WESTERN AUSTRALIA 6005
Telephone: Aust (09) 387 8623
From USA: 011 (619) 387-8623
Facsimile: Aust (09) 387 8689
From USA: 011 (619) 387-8689

☐ **NORTH AMERICAN OFFICE:**
4th Floor, 1407 Market Street,
San Francisco, CALIFORNIA 94103
Telephone: Administration: (415) 621-0338
Facsimile: (415) 863-2686
Orders: USA: 1-800-24-JOKER
Canada: 1-800-54-JOKER
Customer Service: (408) 848-4391
Please respond to office checked ☑

MEDIA RELEASE
from JOKER SOFTWARE INTERNATIONAL

ISSUE DATE: November 2, 1988
EMBARGO UNTIL: IMMEDIATE RELEASE

FOR FURTHER INFORMATION CALL: Peter J. Snow 011-619-387-8623

ANOTHER WONDER FROM DOWN UNDER

The latest import from the land Down Under is sure to attract the attention of entertainment software enthusiasts. Australian-based **Joker Software International** is offering a first prize of **$100,000 cash** as one of more than **1,200 prizes** in a **$200,000 Contest** to mark its entry into the North American market.

CEO Peter J. Snow said from Australia that he understood that the company's new release **"Aussie JOKER POKER"** was the first multi-player P.C. game in history to be simultaneously launched for six different computers.

Part of the promotion involves an **"Aussie JOKER POKER Hall of Fame"** in which purchasers of the game can play at home in a special competition mode written into the software and then send in the highest score they achieved in the hope of being one of the top 25 players in North America.

The Aussie JOKER POKER Contest runs December 1988 through April 1989 with 20 finalists playing for a total of $125,000 cash in a Grand Final at the **Golden Nugget** in Las Vegas on May 20, 1989. Finalists with one guest will receive a round trip coach class from their nearest major airport to Las Vegas and two nights at the Golden Nugget as part of their prize.

Mr. Snow said he was pleased to announce the appointment of **Mindscape, Inc.** of Northbrook, Illinois as distributors of Joker non-violent entertainment software products in the U.S.A. and Canada in conjunction with the launch of Aussie JOKER POKER.

The game offers 90 player capacity, is different to Poker, and was created on an Amiga using True Basic and software tools developed by Joker Software, and then ported to IBM, Macintosh and Atari ST. Complete re-writes were involved for the Apple II and C64/128 versions. The product is the combined work of Joker's Technical and Creative Director, Wolfgang Flatow and Steve Zadarnowski.

Timing is Everything | Peter J Snow OAM

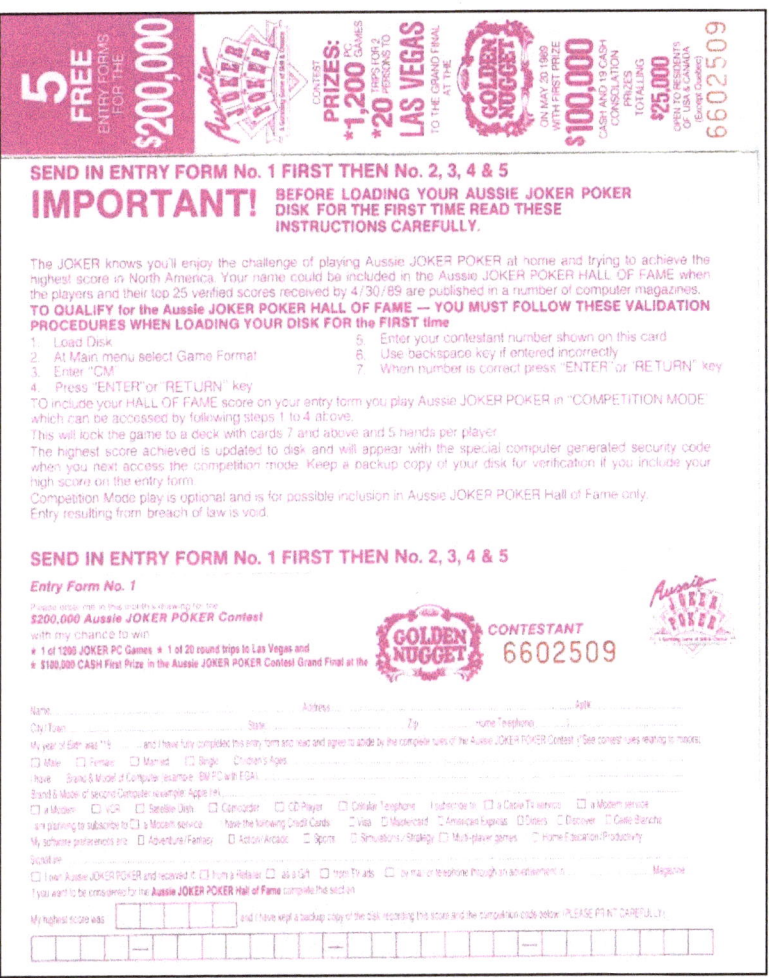

The mailed in coupons would also become the source of a comprehensive database for future marketing purposes.

This would create a loyal target audience for the range of other Joker products to be launched in the following year.

Timing is Everything | Peter J Snow OAM

It was at a time when Mindscape had just secured US$13 million in an Initial Public Offering. We were told that this prevented it providing our sought-after letter of credit for the initial order - so we settled on the next best thing - a Bill of Exchange. A BoE is not quite as good as a Letter of Credit but, as an unconditional promise to pay, it was almost as good. The debt is payable on presentation of a BoE at a financial institution on the nominated date and the debt does not have to be proven at court.

What could possibly go wrong?

Contest laws in Illinois and Florida required us to lodge the total cost of the contest - US$200,000 – in a trust account needing their formal approval for release.

We borrowed AU$257,000 to do so – what with Mindscape's promise of in-store promotion and our full-page ads in computer magazines would guarantee success – so we thought.

As added insurance, we took out a policy with Australia's Export Finance Insurance Corporation to cover possible default and protect the lender of the $257,000. Our bankers said this was a waste of money. Unfortunately, as we would later learn, they were correct in their assessment of EFIC.

To qualify for export grants, the product had to be manufactured in Australia, so the discs, instruction manuals and contest entry forms were produced and inserted into traditional computer game boxes in Perth and then, despite containing 90% of empty space, were air-freighted to Mindscape in Chicago.

Timing is Everything | Peter J Snow OAM

Everything was set. I repeat, what could possibly go wrong?

But our good fortune and prospect of success had run out!

Concerned at the lack of the expected second order and scant sales reports after the initial flurry that had seen more than half of our initial order distributed, I started to call various Electronic Boutique stores around the USA.

This revealed that most stores knew little about Joker Poker and nothing about the $100,000 first prize play-off in Las Vegas - nor was there any point-of-sale or instore promotional material.

As we were to discover later, in the middle of our launch in North America, Mindscape had successfully chewed through most of its $13 million IPO funding and was caught by a glut of games in the retail channel. It was flooded with inventory under its policy of exchanging or taking back slow-moving product.

It was a disaster.

The first of two Bills of Exchange was presented on due date and, as we feared, was not paid. Nor was the second.

Mindscape couldn't (or decided not to) pay its supplier on the other side of the world. So much for our Aussie mate - but as it turned out, he had moved (or been moved) on.

We lodged a claim with our insurers, EFIC, for the whole debt. They declined the claim - contending it was a legal dispute. Despite protestations that there was no dispute, the Bill of Exchange constituted a proven debt, and the real position was Mindscape just couldn't (or wouldn't) pay, EFIC continued to resist and suggested we sue via collection agents or lawyers.

When we explained that our Chicago legal firm required a deposit of US$25,000 (the funds for which we didn't have), EFIC recommended we consider retaining a contingent fee law firm. The going rate for no-win-no-fee was 25% of ultimate proceeds.

With no alternative, we reluctantly entered the contingent fee deal and, after two years of legal argy-bargy, a settlement was reached with our US lawyers taking 25% of the proceeds. It was only about half of the original debt. No wonder they settled quickly on a low-ball figure – they had nothing to lose. I still wonder what would have happened had we been able to bankroll the legal claim – after all, the debt did not need proving.

Thinking we could now prove a claimable loss, we went back to EFIC seeking the shortfall. The claim was refused on the basis that we had *"negotiated a commercial settlement."* The insurer ignored the fact that such negotiations were entered into at its recommendation.

The Bank was right – a total waste of time and money on that insurance which is supposed to help Australian exporters!

So, what then of the contest money on deposit?

Illinois authorities conceded that if the 20 finalists agreed to accept a share of the $140,000 cash component of the $200,000 allocated for prizes, travel and event costs, then they would permit release of the money which was still held in trust.

Many months later, after all 20 had agreed and received $7,000 each to forego a playoff at the Golden Nugget, we received the balance of US$60,000.

Finally, we could claim the AU$200,000 cost of the abandoned contest as an Export Market Development Grant.

Timing is Everything | Peter J Snow OAM

Had everything gone to plan, there would have been no problem, but after two years, claims were now conditional on matching revenue.

Although the legal settlement related to our "product sales", the "commercial" settlement with Mindscape did not qualify as revenue in the current year.

Our savvy export grant adviser confirmed that the then scheme did not specify that the revenue had to be related to the products for which the marketing expenses had been incurred. So "other" export revenue was generated - through the sale of containers of prawns that were shipped to Japan.

The US$140,000 was recovered and the more than anxious private lender repaid in full.

So much for being the first game simultaneously launched on Atari, Amiga, Apple II, Mac, Commodore 64/128 and IBM compatibles.

Our adventure in computer games was over.

LESSONS:
1. DESPITE MY ADVICE NOT TO SPEND PROFITS BEFORE THEY EMEERGED, OUR OVER-CONFIDENT GAME DEVELOPER GOT MARRIED AND BOUGHT A NEW CAR BASED ON HIS ANTICIPATED SHARE OF PROFITS.
   THE LENGTHY DELAY IN RESOLVING MINDSCAPE'S DEBT AND ABSENCE OF THE EXPECTED BONANZA SOURED THE RELATIONSHIP WITH HIM.
2. IT PROVED WHY A SIMPLE 50/50 DEAL IS NEVER A GOOD IDEA - UNLESS THERE ARE CLEAR GUIDELINES TO ADDRESS UNFORTUNATE EVENTS WHEN THE BUSINESS GOES OFF THE RAILS.

3. This was a lesson that was to prove invaluable in subsequent deals.
4. Never accept second best as security unless you have additional alternative and preferably watertight collateral.
5. Don't rely on the "he's a good fella principle, we can trust him" when money is at stake.
6. Take extra care when dealing with customers remote from you. Far away – easily forgotten.
6. Big companies can be ruthless when it comes to self-preservation.

Timing is Everything | Peter J Snow OAM

REVOLUTION ASSISTING EVOLUTION

It never ceases to amaze me that sometimes everything falls into place as if it were destined to be and this story epitomises the sub-title of this book perfectly.

As a new Committee member of a junior football club our five-year old son had joined, I was asked to accompany our Vice President to one of the Subiaco Football Club Junior Council meetings. There had been rumblings within junior club circles over the apparently less than democratic conduct of these meetings chaired by a Subiaco Football Club Director. He was said to rule by the *"my way or the highway"* principle with significant disregard for junior clubs' input. Being well versed in chairmanship and meeting procedure from my Jaycee training, I was sceptical of this claim but not prepared for the less than warm greeting: *"Welcome. You can come in, you can listen - but you cannot speak".* It appeared that the rumblings of discontent had indeed well justified.

The proceedings certainly supported what I had been told to anticipate.

With rapid expansion in Perth's northern suburbs, the growing number of junior football clubs were affiliated with one of three different state league clubs - Subiaco, Claremont or West Perth.

Shire Councillor (ultimately Mayor) Dr Wayne Bradshaw was also called upon as a junior football umpire and was keen to consolidate all clubs in the Shire of Wanneroo into one league.

Timing is Everything | Peter J Snow OAM

There were already 131 junior teams within the Shire, so the idea had merit as some parents were faced with up to an hour's travel for early games. This affected more than 2,500 children and nearly 2,000 families and a 15% annual growth rate expected.

The junior clubs and Shire officials met to devise a game plan. I was enlisted to chair the steering committee.

A constitution for what was to be *Wanneroo Junior Football League Inc.* - with each club having one vote and a "parent" club (if any) having a non-voting delegate. The operational plan called for a part-time league manager and a two-year $20,000 funding package as well as scheduling games on 26 ovals and reserves.

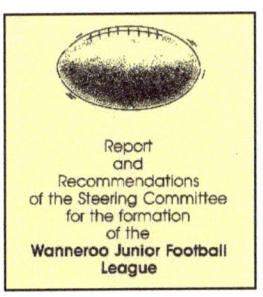

Report and Recommendations of the Steering Committee for the formation of the Wanneroo Junior Football League

Almost as if the fickle finger of fate had intervened or the state league's hierarchy had reached a similar conclusion to the junior clubs and realigned the junior zones.

Overnight, all clubs in the Wanneroo Shire were now zoned to Subiaco Football Club.

How fortuitous!

It was the right time for change ... for the better!

Chairing a meeting attended for the first time by Subiaco's President and General Manager proved to be a challenge worthy of Henry Kissinger.

Timing is Everything | Peter J Snow OAM

The meeting nearly ended when Subiaco's representatives insisted that the Subiaco name replace Wanneroo, rejected any suggestion of funding and demanded voting rights. That approach resulted in one angry club delegate exploding with: *"you've got nothing, you give nothing, and you want everything – you make me sick".*

This prompted the Subiaco delegation to head for the exit. However, with supreme diplomacy, the imminent disaster was diffused. As a compromise, the name *Subiaco's Wanneroo Junior Football League Inc* was agreed and Subiaco Football Club committed to $10,000 of funding over the first two years for the "democratically independent" new body.

After a slightly shaky start, the new parent-juniors relationship blossomed.

The league was to evolve into the *North Suburban Junior Football League Inc.* which was one of the largest and most successful in Australia. It boasted more than three thousand young players before being dismantled in an overall restructure of regional football.

The term: *"if it ain't broke, don't fix it"* had obviously not been grasped by those in power.

LESSON: Logic and revolution can help democratic evolution

A CAPITAL(ISER) IDEA

As a first-time world traveller and attendee at a Jaycees World Congress, I made it my business to attend as many seminars and training sessions as possible – between visits to Amsterdam's tourist attractions and a final function among the priceless works of art in the Van Gogh Museum.

One such "Community Project" seminar featured a bank-sponsored investment game from Scotland called "Capitaliser". It aimed to educate high school students about the workings of the stock market and the free enterprise system.

I gathered up the offered promotional leaflets to follow up the idea on my return to Australia but my attempts to extract further information from our Scottish counterparts were met with resounding silence. Nevertheless, I put the concept to my own chapter, Fremantle Jaycees.

My enthusiasm for an educational community project that we could better than the Scots was shared.

A committee was formed and project plan developed.

First step was to gain access to the students. This we did via the Economics Teachers' Association whose then President was Greg Hancock, an Economics teacher.

Hancock relished the idea of a practical approach to commercial education. Next, we enlisted Perth Stock Exchange and weekday evening paper - the Daily News.

The concept involved teams of up to five students researching a list of shares and selecting a portfolio from a range of industrial and mining stocks. Stocks could be bought and sold periodically with the winners being the syndicate achieving the biggest gain in their portfolio value over the period of the game starting with a notional "stake" of $50,000.

The committee's role was to verify calculations and feed progress results to the Daily News that published a "Leaders Board".

In the first year, 800 students participated and won Fremantle Jaycees the award for *Best Commercial Education Project in the World* at the JCI World Congress in Johannesburg, South Africa.

The success created national interest and, with the Australian Stock Exchange yet to be established, Share Game Committees comprising representatives of Jaycees, local paper, state Stock Exchange and Economics teachers were formed in each state.

In a day when online technology was a mere thought bubble, the prospect of manually marking thousands of investment decisions on a frequent basis was daunting.

Bruce Hunt, a member of Swan Jaycees was then an IT specialist working in the state's racing information hub and offered to develop computerised processing technology for the thousands of investment decisions being made on a regular basis.

The WA Institute of Technology (Curtin University) volunteered to scan the coded printed OCR entry forms from all over Australia on its DECsystem-10 computer.

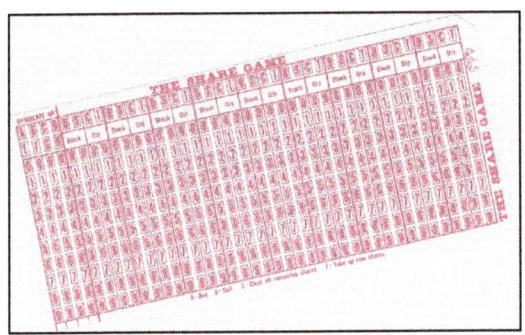

And so it was that 13,000 students from all over Australia participated with this number building to 50,000 annually over the next decade - with two games running each year.

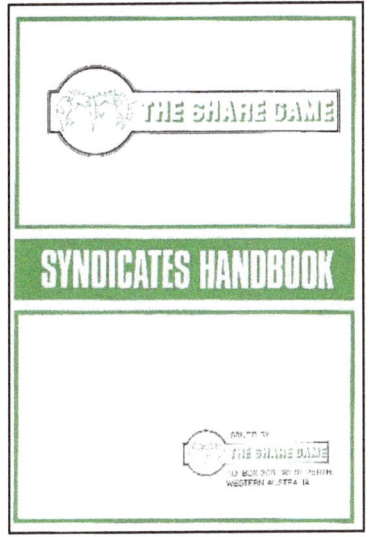

Ease of online access would encourage entry and revolutionise processing of entry, investment decisions and valuations.

Only problem was, the software development was at risk at a critical time because Hunt had a money problem. He was facing a potential second fraud charge (didn't learn from the first). I reluctantly and foolishly lent him the required bailout with a promise of weekly repayments and a formal acknowledgement of debt. The software was successfully finished and, soon after, so did repayments. Hunt disappeared interstate. He reappeared years later promoting a seminar as state manager of a computer firm. Confronted by my debt collector, Hunt agreed to pay the debt but stalled sufficiently to resort to the Statute of Limitations to deny payment. Obviously, he had forgotten the *Jaycee Creed*.

On the bright side, nearly 50 years since it started, and although the Jaycees organisation is no longer involved, the Share Market game is still conducted by the Australian Stock Exchange. In that time, more than two million students have participated.

POSTSCRIPT: Greg Hancock became the Public Relations Spokesman for the Perth Stock Exchange and, ultimately, a successful Stockbroker, capital raiser and public company non-executive director.

So, who says games can't change lives (and careers)?

LESSON:
1. THERE IS NOTHING WRONG WITH PLAGIARISM – IF YOU DO IT BETTER!
2. DON'T FALL FOR STORIES WHERE PREVIOUS DISHONESTY IS ADMITTED

SOLID FOUNDATIONS AND A VITAL INVESTMENT

As part of my increasing focus on service to the community, in 1975, I developed the idea of a spin-off of the state Jaycees organisation aimed at undertaking larger community projects. It would also be suitable for ongoing projects - management of which would not be inhibited by the annual changeover of Jaycee chapter office bearers designed to give young members experience in different roles on committees.

Jaycees State President Ron Raynor liked the concept and it was unanimously endorsed by the 1975 Western Australian Jaycees State Conference.

Ron and I co-founded *The Jaycees Community Foundation Inc* as an incorporated not-for-profit association. Managed by a board of "senior" Jaycee members, it also had a Benevolent Fund to which tax-deductible donations could be made.

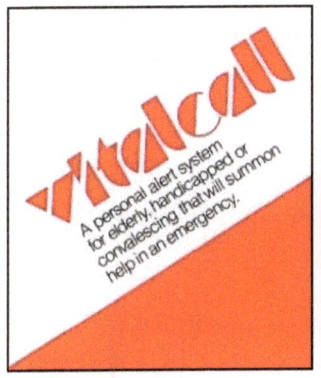
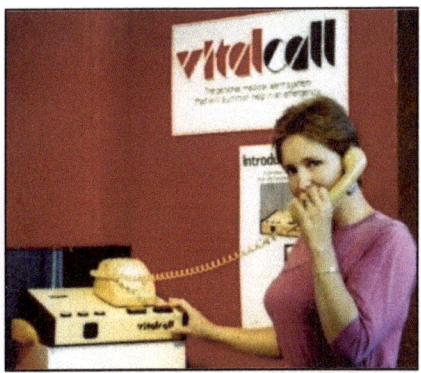

The Foundation's first major community project was to pioneer computerised medical alert systems in Western Australia.

It obtained the state rights to *VitalCall* – a system allowing elderly and those with a disability to remain in the comfort of their own home instead of being placed in care.

It was a great idea that would have a beneficial financial impact for government by reducing pressure on the health care system.

However, it was a marketing enigma.

The primary user market was the elderly – most of whom considered this new-fangled electronic device as unnecessary as they were not "old enough" or they considered the daily pressing of a check-in button an intrusion into their lives – an obstacle faced by many potential customers seeking the system for aging parents.

Despite this marketing barrier, the business grew to 163 clients while the Foundation was lobbying government to adopt the idea statewide and provide it as a free service.

In the absence of any advice to the Foundation, a government tender to do just that opened and closed.

The first we knew was that a national security service *Chubb* in conjunction with a disability services provider *Silver Chain* had been granted the contract.

With the majority of our 163 clients now qualifying for a free service, we had no option but to recommend that they avail themselves of the government's benevolence and cancel their contract with the Foundation.

Timing is Everything | Peter J Snow OAM

The letters of appreciation from many users and their families softened the financial blow to the Foundation.

At 140 users the service had reached break-even point and at 163 was starting to recoup the establishment losses when the free service was introduced.

In retrospect the loss was still a good community investment.

LESSON:
1. MONITOR POTENTIAL CHANGES IN YOUR INDUSTRY.
2. DON'T REGRET A LOSS IF THE COMMUNITY BENEFITS.

ONE MAN'S JOURNEY

Driving home one evening an interview on talk-back radio was of interest. The Western Australian Children's Choir was seeking sponsorship.

By pure co-incidence (or maybe fate) the choir had been the half-time entertainment at a football game my wife and I had attended the week before. They were great.

Thinking it may be something our Foundation might have an interest in, I rang the radio station and left my details to be passed on to the choir management.

The result was a visit from the Choir's Musical Director, George Fay. I remembered him from his days as a member of "The Four Kinsmen" a successful musical comedy group from years past.

We canvassed the idea of the Foundation sponsoring the upgrade of the choir's annual recording to CD format when George made a startling admission. Apologising for frequently wiping his mouth, he admitted to Motor Neurone Disease that had been diagnosed two years before. Aware that the average lifespan after diagnosis of this incurable and debilitating disease was four years, I realised that I was looking at a man for whom every moment was extremely valuable.

But George had an idea. He wanted to raise money for research so that there was hope for those faced with a similar predicament to his in the future.

He would prevail on his friends in the music profession to donate a track for a compilation CD with proceeds of sales going to the MND associations (of which there was one in each state).

The Foundation relished the idea, and after George confirmed the donation of tracks from his colleagues, we sought royalty waivers from copyright owners of the selected songs. All but one agreed to our request.

The Australian Broadcasting Commission provided its studio for the Children's Choir to record backing harmonies for three of the stars' songs and Sony produced the CDs at a significant discount.

My request for the Children's Choir to perform John Farnham's – *"Playing to Win"* - was agreed to. It was a theme song for me.

Despite his decreasing capabilities, George Fay painted profiles of all contributors to form the cover art-work and the Foundation printed the tribute booklet insert.

American Express carried a promotional piece with its monthly statements and a national magazine published the story behind the CD. George's careful selection of tracks indeed made "One Man's Journey" an appropriate legacy that delivered more than $35,000 to Motor Neurone Disease associations across Australia.

The project went on to receive a JCI Asia-Pacific Award for the Best Project for Assistance to the Handicapped.

RIGHT:
Foundation Deputy Chairman Neville Clare presents an initial cheque to George Fay's widow for WA's MND Association

RIGHT:
Albany Mayor Alison Goode and Jaycees Community Foundation Chairman Peter Snow with the JCI Asia-Pacific Award for the One Man's Journey Project

LESSONS:

1. NEVER STOP THINKING OF OTHERS – EVEN IF YOUR END IS IN SIGHT.
2. MOST PEOPLE AND BUSINESSES ARE WILLING TO HELP OR CONTRIBUTE IF THE OBJECTIVE IS WORTHY AND/OR WILL REDUCE SUFFERING.
3. IF YOU DON'T ASK – YOU WILL NEVER RECEIVE.

VENTURING FORWARD

While it could be said that story about the final story – about the gift of Australia's last derelict whaling station to the Jaycees Community Foundation - stands alone as remarkable – it is not. It had other unpredicted consequences.

With me playing rugby at Christ Church I had little to do with a hockey-playing classmate, Bruce Gallash (three weeks my senior), until we both ended up as Board members of Rainbow Coast Tourism Directorate Inc – the Great Southern's regional tourism body.

I was representing tourist attractions and Bruce, as Chair of the Shire of Denmark's Finance Committee, was representing local government.

We hit it off and, when Bruce moved back to Perth from his idyllic paradise on the Irwin Inlet near Peaceful Bay on the south-coast, he rented an office next to mine.

The relationship grew and he bought a house and adjoining office complex in Evandale Street, Floreat – a leafy western suburb – in which we established a boutique venture capital firm – *The Evandale House Group.*

This evolved into an extraordinary, 15-year business partnership and friendship that endures today.

To avoid any conflict of interest, I folded my company - *Venture Capital Corporation International Pty Ltd* - into the business.

Timing is Everything | Peter J Snow OAM

Bruce is a visionary and some of the projects we syndicated were innovative and based on his remarkably creative mind.

My role was syndication and development of the appropriate mechanisms to deliver a fair reward for risks encountered – remembering that a very small percentage of start-ups achieve success (or actually survive).

Overall, we did better than average and, had fate not intervened, it would have been a lot better!

A MEMBER OF THE EVANDALE HOUSE GROUP

E.H.G. PTY LTD
ACN 076 342 473
AS TRUSTEE FOR
THE E.H.G. UNIT TRUST
T/AS THE EVANDALE HOUSE GROUP

MEMBERS OF
THE EVANDALE HOUSE GROUP
INCLUDE:

AQUACULTURE INVESTMENTS INTERNATIONAL LIMITED
GALLASH NOMINEES PTY LTD
   AS TRUSTEE FOR THE GALLASH FAMILY INVESTMENT TRUST
HOOFLON INTERNATIONAL PTY LTD
HWL INTERNATIONAL PTY LTD
MERCURA TECHNOLOGIES PTY LTD
O.C. GLOBAL MANAGEMENT PTY LTD
   AS TRUSTEE FOR THE VENTURE MANAGEMENT TRUST
PANDAROO INTERNATIONAL PTY LTD
PLUTORA PTY LTD
   AS TRUSTEE FOR THE M&M TRUST
PRISM PACKAGING PTY LTD
RED RABBIT PTY LTD
SOFTWARE INTERNATIONAL PTY LTD
   AS TRUSTEE FOR THE TVI TRUST
TRAVELORA PTY LTD
TRAVEL VISION INTERNATIONAL PTY LTD
   AND WHOLLY OWNED SUBSIDIARIES
   TRAVEL VISION (AMERICAS) INC (INCORPORATED IN DELAWARE, U.S.A.)
   TRAVEL VISION (ASIA) LIMITED (INCORPORATED IN HONG KONG)
   TRAVEL VISION (AUSTRALIA) PTY LTD
   TRAVEL VISION (EUROPE) LIMITED (INCORPORATED IN THE U.K.)
TYCHE PTY LTD
   AS TRUSTEE FOR THE MANAGEMENT & MARKETING TRUST
   TRADING AS
   M&M LICENCE MANAGEMENT & MARKETING
VENTURE CAPITAL CORPORATION
   INTERNATIONAL PTY LTD
VISCOUNT NOMINEES PTY LTD
   AS TRUSTEE FOR THE VISCOUNT TRUST

ACTIVITIES

THE E.H.G. UNIT TRUST WAS ESTABLISHED IN 1996 AS AN UMBRELLA ENTITY FOR THE EXPANDING JOINT INTERESTS OF THE GALLASH AND SNOW FAMILIES. THE TRUST TRADES UNDER THE REGISTERED BUSINESS NAME *THE EVANDALE HOUSE GROUP* AND OPERATES FROM THE GROUP'S CORPORATE OFFICE IN FLOREAT, WESTERN AUSTRALIA OWNED BY THE GALLASH FAMILY.

GROUP ENTITIES ARE INVOLVED IN A NUMBER OF DIVERSIFIED FIELDS INCLUDING INFORMATION TECHNOLOGY, AQUACULTURE, EDUCATIONAL MATERIALS MARKETING, PUBLISHING AND COSMETICS MANUFACTURING.

A MAJOR PART OF THE GROUP'S BUSINESS IS IN THE SYNDICATION OF PRIVATE INVESTMENT IN PROJECTS WHERE MANAGEMENT AND MARKETING ARE ESSENTIAL ELEMENTS, PARTICULARLY WHERE THERE IS INTERNATIONAL POTENTIAL.

THE GROUP'S JOINT VENTURE AND STRATEGIC ALLIANCE PHILOSOPHY HAS SEEN IT EXPAND INTO CHINA - THE EMERGING MARKET OF THE NEXT MILLENNIUM AND ITS SEED CAPITAL FUNDING PROGRAM HAS ALREADY BORNE FRUIT THROUGH CAREFUL SELECTION OF PROJECTS WITH POTENTIAL FROM THE MANY OPPORTUNITIES THAT ARE PRESENTED.

APART FROM ITS INVESTMENT ROLE, E.H.G. UNDERTAKES SPECIAL CONSULTANCY AND PROJECT CO-ORDINATION ROLES THROUGH THE RETENTION OF APPROPRIATELY QUALIFIED PERSONNEL.

TRAVEL VISION – A VISION TOO FAR … AHEAD

They say timing is everything and Bruce's idea for *Travel Vision* was, unfortunately, 10 years ahead of its time.

His original thought of converting the classified ads in the Sunday paper to an online marketplace (which has since become a reality as eBay and GumTree) evolved into the genesis of an idea to revolutionise distribution of information for the travel industry.

At the time, accommodation bookings in distant locations relied mainly on the knowledge of travel agents and word of mouth recommendation or brochures.

Space limitations obviously prevented brochure storage for the range of exotic locations many agents promoted.

There must be a better way … and there was!

The idea of offering hotel images electronically as well as dynamic data such as prices and availability was an obvious answer. But remember, this was well before internet speeds allowed live-streaming of images.

How could the images and other static information be displayed?

CDs were the answer. The only problem was that most Travel Agents who used computers for travel and accommodation bookings did not have a computer with a CD Drive and screens displaying in colour - but that could be addressed.

Timing is Everything | Peter J Snow OAM

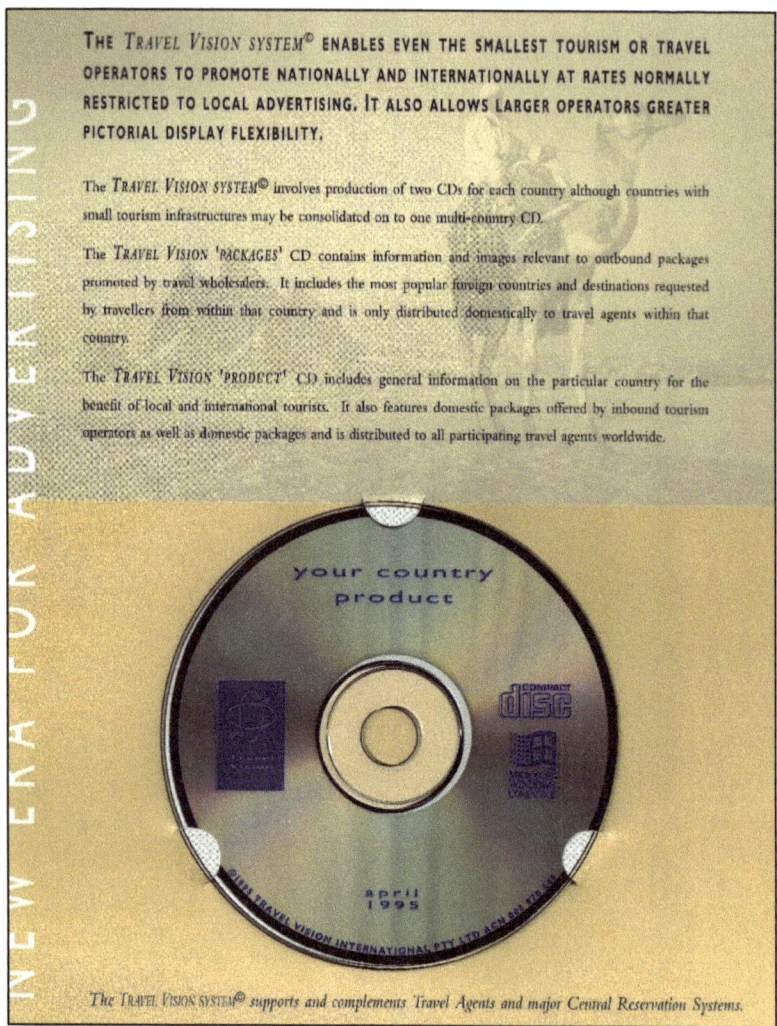

THE *TRAVEL VISION SYSTEM*© **ENABLES EVEN THE SMALLEST TOURISM OR TRAVEL OPERATORS TO PROMOTE NATIONALLY AND INTERNATIONALLY AT RATES NORMALLY RESTRICTED TO LOCAL ADVERTISING. IT ALSO ALLOWS LARGER OPERATORS GREATER PICTORIAL DISPLAY FLEXIBILITY.**

The *TRAVEL VISION SYSTEM*© involves production of two CDs for each country although countries with small tourism infrastructures may be consolidated on to one multi-country CD.

The *TRAVEL VISION* 'PACKAGES' CD contains information and images relevant to outbound packages promoted by travel wholesalers. It includes the most popular foreign countries and destinations requested by travellers from within that country and is only distributed domestically to travel agents within that country.

The *TRAVEL VISION* 'PRODUCT' CD includes general information on the particular country for the benefit of local and international tourists. It also features domestic packages offered by inbound tourism operators as well as domestic packages and is distributed to all participating travel agents worldwide.

The *TRAVEL VISION SYSTEM*© *supports and complements Travel Agents and major Central Reservation Systems.*

Travel Vision International Pty Ltd was established with nearly $4 million of backing through the granting of territory licences covering various countries to investors recognising the potential.

Timing is Everything | Peter J Snow OAM

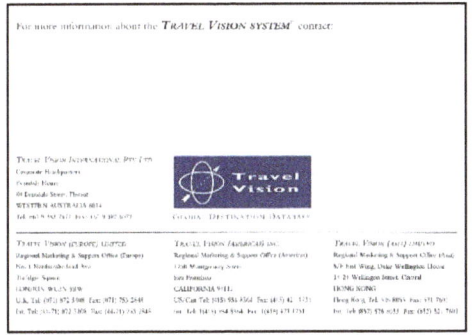

Subsidiaries with serviced offices were set up in London, Hong Kong and San Francisco from which our marketing team could operate – all based on a well-researched Global Business Plan.

The idea was simple – licence areas in which a sub-licensee could generate advertising revenue by selling accommodation providers on the virtues of electronic advertising globally.

It would be cheaper than printing and distributing brochures – and while the pictures would be static on CDs, the information on prices and availability could be dynamically updated online.

The aim would be to sell country sub-licences (on behalf of investor licensees) to marketers within those countries.

An upfront sub-licence fee and a percentage of advertising revenue from the accommodation providers would sustain the global business.

Investor licensees would receive a return from the up-front sub-licence fee and royalties based on the sub-licensee's revenue.

Timing is Everything | Peter J Snow OAM

THE PRESENT. The travel industry currently uses printed matter as its main information source. Production and distribution costs are considerable and increasing – limiting both presentation quality and the quantity of advertisers' information available. Insufficient brochure production and distribution results in product not being available in the marketplace while excess leads to dumping of surplus brochures after expiry date.

THE FUTURE. Electronic advertising presents tourism, leisure, and travel information in a highly cost-effective and efficient manner - reducing the reliance of the industry on expensive brochures and the associated production and distribution problems. Electronic information can be readily updated whenever required - at a fraction of the cost of printed material. The *TRAVEL VISION SYSTEM*® is the electronic brochure of the future - now.

Travel Vision
GLOBAL DESTINATION DATABASE

NEW TECHNOLOGY. The *TRAVEL VISION SYSTEM*® provides a high quality 'Pictorial Global Destination Database' offering instant access to current information selected on a range of nominated criteria and supports it with large, high resolution colour images. The *TRAVEL VISION SYSTEM*® uses the latest CD-ROM and image compression technology.

The *TRAVEL VISION SYSTEM*® offers

BENEFITS FOR TRAVEL AGENTS
- Complements current agency structures
- Better, instant point-of-sale information
- Enhances 'selling' features of destinations and products
- Improves income potential through wider product range
- User-friendly system improves current booking techniques
- Instant multi-lingual and multi-currency information
- Client database facility for record and direct marketing purposes
- System prompts client to make product decisions
- Increases consultant's product knowledge
- Current updated product prices from participating advertisers
- Information can be printed out
- Faster handling of telephone enquiries

NEW ENHANCED FEATURES INCLUDE A COMPLETE AGENCY SOFTWARE PACKAGE COMPRISING:
- Itinerary planner
- Client database program
- Marketing module

BENEFITS FOR ADVERTISERS IN THE TRAVEL AND TOURISM INDUSTRY
- A neutral information service
- Complements major Central Reservation Systems
- A low cost global advertising alternative
- Unlimited pictorial display availability
- Current product information always available at booking source
- Product incentive opportunities for increased revenue

BENEFITS FOR THE TRAVELLER
- Better comprehensive information
- Quickly identifies products meeting desired criteria
- Speeds up decision making
- Greater visual display and impact than brochures offer

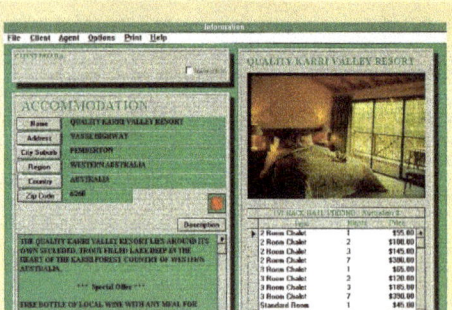

The *TRAVEL VISION SYSTEM*® offers:
- More booking opportunities
- A Design allowing for instant access to Travel Agents existing Central Reservation System
- Instant language conversion
- Instant price conversion to local currency
- Weekly pricing update option for products

TRAVEL VISION'S CDs

The 'PACKAGES' CD contains information on outbound packages to popular foreign destinations

The Travel Vision System would offer global advertising for a fraction of the cost of traditional advertising and brochure production.

The added advantage over a printed brochure is that data such as prices and availability could be updated instantly. Once signed up, annual renewals were likely to occur and revenues escalate as more providers sought global distribution. It was all based on simple marketing economics and first-mover advantage.

The territory sub-licensee would be required to provide an updated CD master every six months and contribute to the production of CDs for that territory which would then be distributed to travel agents globally.

After lengthy negotiations, the terms of a Memorandum of Understanding were agreed with the Geneva-based Société Internationale de Télécommunications Aéronautiques (SITA – the world's leading Central Reservation System used by the majority of the world's airlines). This dealt with the dynamic updating of data and availability issues relevant to most hotels and resorts.

Next was equipment. With our syndicated funding starting to diminish and one sub-licensee (for Ireland) signed up, it was critical to establish a partnership of sorts with a major computer supplier. Success required travel agents to have computers with CD drives to be able to screen the CDs upon which the hotel product could be displayed – in full colour.

Timing is Everything | Peter J Snow OAM

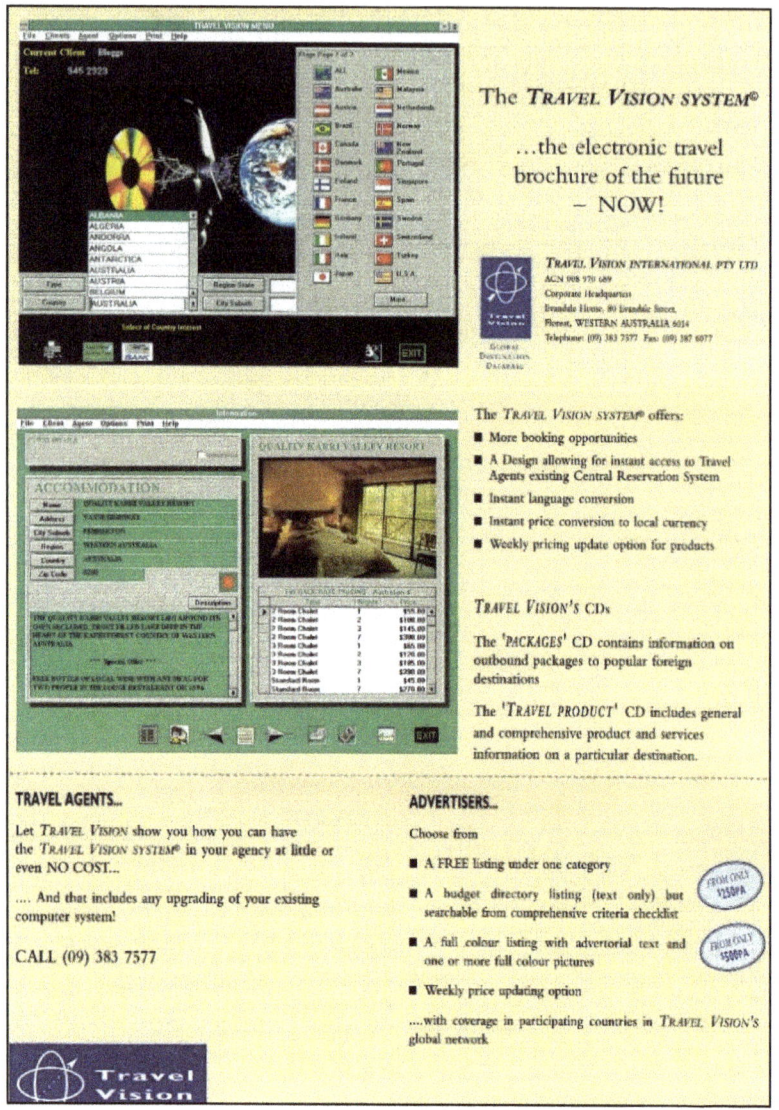

Negotiations were well advanced with IBM for a global supply and funding deal.

Fate intervened.

As Bruce was actually in the air flying to New York to finalise our joint-venture, IBM's Senior Vice President with whom he was dealing, had a stroke and never recovered.

Without his direct involvement neither did our deal.

It was (and is) a great concept.

Today, you can recognise the Travel Vision concept as the multi-billion-dollar company known as Booking.com.

As I have often learnt - *Timing is Everything*!

But EHG went on with a range of projects with varying degrees of success (or lack thereof).

But they were interesting times and great fun.

LESSONS:
1. ALWAYS HAVE CONTINGENCY PLAN B … AND CONTINGENCY PLAN C.
2. IT WILL ALWAYS TAKE LONGER AND COST MORE THAN YOU THINK.
3. WHEN DEALING WITH CORPORATES TRY AND ENSURE THAT THERE IS A SECONDARY CONTACT IN CASE, FOR WHATEVER REASON, YOUR MAIN CONTACT IS NOT THERE TOMORROW.
4. APPLY THE PRINCIPLE THAT WHAT MIGHT GO WRONG WILL GO WRONG.
5. IF YOU ARE USING THE FIRST MOVER PRINCIPLE – MOVE FAST.
6. UNDER COMMIT AND OVER DELIVER ON PROMISES.
7. KEEP BACKERS INFORMED AT EVERY STAGE – OBSTACLES AND WINS.

ON THE HOOF – LITERALLY!

A molecular scientist by the name of Dr Peter Kay sought our advice on a product he had invented. Like most successful products, it solved a problem ... this one was for horses.

We quickly learnt that, during work, continuous flexion of a dehydrated hoof will cause cracks, fissures and crumbling of the lower regions of the hoof. Contrastingly, if the hoof wall contains excess moisture, it becomes too soft and impact pressures transmitted to softer tissues and joints can cause lameness. Poor re-shoeing can also allow water absorption.

Excessive water gain or loss from the hoof wall is reduced by a naturally occurring waterproof coating called the stratum tectorium. This is easily lost and Peter had a more practical and convenient solution to maintain hoof health than other options.

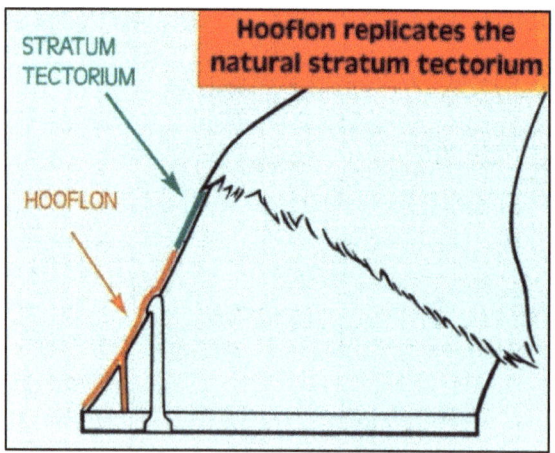
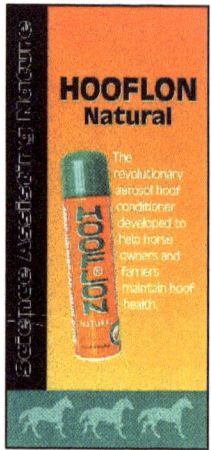

Timing is Everything | Peter J Snow OAM

The solution was Hooflon in an aerosol spray can. No messy grease-like paste to apply and, unlike other noisy aerosols that made horses skittish, this was a low-noise aerosol pack.

We agreed to a joint-venture with Peter in the form of *Hooflon International Pty Ltd* and promptly negotiated a licensing deal with a prominent equine supply group in New Zealand.

Seemed to be too good to be true ... and it was!

But not because of the product – those using it swore by its effectiveness - it was how it could be delivered safely to willing customers that was the problem.

It was a time when risks with aerosol cans in planes became an issue and Australia Post also banned them in the mail. It suffered a similar fate in New Zealand. Easy to ship them by sea but once landed, how could they be delivered to the customer.

It became too hard, so we happily "donated" our shares to the inventor to allow him to come up with the answer.

LESSONS:
1. IT IS ONE THING TO HAVE A GREAT PRODUCT BUT MORE IMPORTANT TO BE ABLE TO DELIVER IT TO THE CUSTOMER.
2. RECOGNISE WHEN YOU SHOULD MOVE ON – VALUE THE EXPERIENCE.

ORGANICALLY BAD

Do you ever wish you had never heard of what appears to be a great deal?

Well, this is one of those stories.

One of our potentially internationally successful deals had gone off the rails. Through bitter experience, we had been wise enough to be able to intervene via a charge we held over the half interest in a joint-venture company and unit trust that our investor syndicate didn't own.

The charge was part of our security for a loan to the Inventor's company ... about which you will hear more later.

With our General Manager denied access to the factory, and the project at an impasse, the decision had been made to use our charge to resolve the matter by appointing a Receiver.

I then had to fly to Albany to attend the funeral of the manager of the *Jaycees Community Foundation's* whaling station project who had tragically died in an aircraft accident.

Although I was one of two Directors representing our investor syndicate on the joint-venture Board and despite the gravity of the situation, the funeral was not something I could miss.

The Receiver was to serve his papers about the time the funeral service was to conclude when I received a message to call my business partner urgently.

Bruce, my fellow investor-group representative Director, Rob Collins and the appointed Receiver, accountant Kevin Judge, had arrived at the factory.

As Kevin was attempting to serve papers and access the factory, a criminal lawyer by the name of Geoff Vickridge (also a Director – but nominated by the inventor), had come charging out of the factory office and into the startled Receiver - pushing him back into bushes, tearing his suit and narrowly missing smashing his head on a tree stump. Vickridge had retreated into the office and locked the door. Obviously realising that an assault charge may jeopardise his professional future, the repentant lawyer re-emerged and ushered the stunned Receiver into the office – but on his own. After witnessing the assault and fearing for the accountant's safety, the others had called the police.

Having had just an hour or so briefing that Friday morning, the Receiver was in a quandary as to who to believe.

With Vickridge promising replacement of the damaged suit and arrangements made to address issues on Monday, the police departed, and the dust settled ... but not for long!

A mere day later, the factory was the subject of an arson attack and the fire brigade had cause to call the police when they discovered Cannabis plants growing at the back of the factory.

What a surprise it was to find that business records and part of the factory where containers of fertiliser were stored were the worst affected by the fire. And things went from bad to worse.

In the confusion and speed of events, the Receiver's insurers had not been notified of his appointment nor of the fire until well after the required notification period. They denied the claim. Now reliance on the project's original insurers had to be sought – but what was the claim?

While the containers were owned by the company, the fertiliser mix it contained was owned by the inventor until it had been paid for by the joint-venture company – which hadn't happened.

Ownership had to be determined by the Supreme Court.

With that resolved in the company's favour, eventually the company's original insurer processed the claim – but the joy of success was to be short-lived.

The day notification of approval of the claim was received was the day the insurer, FAI (now part of HIH Insurances) went into provisional liquidation.

The HIH collapse was the subject of a federal government bailout (and a judicial enquiry) but it was many months before discounted compensation was received by the Receiver.

So, you ask, what is the back story of these unfortunate events?

Well, it went like this.

Our corporate lawyer's cousin had a client who had been subject to some "issues" in the past but had developed some organic fertiliser that was too good to be true.

One should always remember the old saying *"If it sounds too good to be true, then it probably is!"*

Always keeping an open mind and willing to consider giving people a second chance, Bruce Gallash and I, accompanied by our corporate lawyer, attended a preliminary meeting with his lawyer cousin.

The examples of the success of his client's magic organic mix of herbs and spices were astounding.

The state's major sporting oval and the capital city's floral gardens were impressive examples that would excite investors. It naturally piqued our interest in learning more.

Apart from an immediate need for cash to settle creditors (including the Australian Tax Office for unpaid staff taxes and superannuation), the main "issue" was that the inventor had spent some time at the Governor's pleasure. He was, as it was put to us, the "patsy" for thwarting a public tender system for which the "primary high-profile beneficiary" and relevant witnesses had suffered severe memory loss at the court hearing.

Being aware of the questionable activities of the named party, and possibly blinkered by what could become a global success, we were content to give the inventor a "second chance" – but with safe-guards put in place to protect our potential investor syndicate. As with Colonel Sanders and Coca Cola we understood the inventor's reluctance to disclose the formula to his concoction – but we knew it worked – or so it appeared.

So, we were content to have the "recipe" cut in half and the two halves deposited in safety deposit boxes in two separate banks - with strict escrow conditions.

We raised $3 million from investors of which $300,000 was lent to the inventor's company to enable it to clear debt. Having learnt from bitter experience of previous 50/50 deals, we took a charge over the inventor's company's 50% interest in the joint-venture with various trigger clauses.

[We were to learn later that the $300,000 in loan funds never reached their intended destinations. Like butter on a hot frying pan the funds barely touched the sides on their way elsewhere - leaving creditors lamenting.]

The joint-venture company *Organo Culture International Pty Ltd* (and unit trust) Board was me, Rob Collins (a well-qualified accountant and non-executive Director), criminal lawyer Geoff Vickridge and the wife of the inventor representing him (as his history prevented him holding corporate office).

With Roger Crook, a dour and well qualified former senior executive of a global chemical manufacturer and distributor recruited as General Manager and a clearly defined Business Plan in operation, things looked very promising.

Crook was in the final stages of negotiation with the fourth largest fertiliser manufacturer in Europe when, mysteriously, the deal disintegrated.

Subsequent investigation hinted at it having been white-anted by a third party at the behest of the inventor when he apparently realised that there was the prospect of "real" money to flow to the joint-venture.

It appeared that a personality flaw called greed had overtaken the concept of 50% of something is better than 100% of nothing and the risk of legal drama was conveniently overlooked. The golden goose principle was indeed still alive and well.

The revelations of some behind-the-scenes manipulations and downright dishonesty brought the matter to a head.

General Manager Crook being refused factory entry was the final straw. The decision was made to protect the interests of our investors by triggering the default clause under the registered charge we held for the original $300,000 loan.

While I could have chaired a meeting of investors, but with the inventor and Vickridge attending, we decided to bring in an independent lawyer to chair the meeting.

It proved to be a disaster as the "independent" chair succeeded in alienating many of the investors with his rapier-like tongue not dealing with investors' questions appropriately.

As a result, the confused investors sided with the smooth-talking (and now demure) inventor, accepting an absurd half-baked proposal that they would ultimately come to regret.

With that decision went their total investment.

Many moons later, we were not surprised to see a liquidator's advertisement seeking expressions of interest for 100,000 litres of organic fertiliser.

What a coincidence!

LESSONS:
1. DON'T TAKE A DEAL THAT LOOKS TOO GOOD TO BE TRUE. IT PROBABLY IS … BUT IF YOU DO HAVE CAUSE TO GIVE IT A SECOND LOOK - AT LEAST REVIEW IT CAREFULLY… JUST IN CASE IT IS THAT RARE GEM WORTH PAIN AND AGGRAVATION.
2. SECOND CHANCES ARE FINE, BUT DOUBLE YOUR DUE DILIGENCE AND BE TOTALLY SATISFIED THAT THE "ABERRATION" WAS NOT BASED ON AN INBUILT TRAIT OF DISHONESTY OR GREED.
3. WHERE YOU HAVE MORE TO LOSE THAN THE PROPONENT LEAN ON THE SIDE OF PASSING UNLESS YOU CAN STRUCTURE AN ARRANGEMENT WHERE THE PROPONENT HAS A LOT TO LOSE – NOT JUST YOUR MONEY.
4. HIRE THE RIGHT PEOPLE TO RUN THE BUSINESS – INVENTORS ARE RARELY SUCCESSFUL AT ALSO RUNNING A BUSINESS WELL.
5. WHEN THE FERTILISER HITS THE FAN – MAKE SURE YOU HAVE PLAN B … AND PLAN C.

Timing is Everything | Peter J Snow OAM

LITTLE FRIENDS - A LESSON IN CONTROLLING THE SUPPLY CHAIN

Always on the look-out for interesting business opportunities, a "for sale" advertisement for a pet supplies wholesale business called Poland Wholesale attracted my attention.

The price was just stock value - which should have been a warning sign - but I recall that there was a justifiable reason for the vendor's exit and so applied my mind to what seemed to be a bargain. Australians increasing spend on everything associated with domestic animals should surely be a growth area – and that prediction has become today's reality.

The customer base of the wholesaler was retail pet and aquarium stores to which it supplied pet accessories such as cages, toys, pet beds, aquariums and related equipment - rather than the riskier area of perishable food lines. Mark-ups were substantial.

I floated the idea with a good Jaycee friend, Garry Leighton, who shared my enthusiasm. Having significant existing business commitments, we both saw it as a silent partner investment.

All it needed was the right person to manage it and its two staff.

During my period as accountant at Mayday Hire, Managing Director, Warren Jones had a trusty lieutenant, Len Hunt, as his General Manager. Len had always impressed me as a reliable, meticulous and efficient administrator.

I was aware that the trauma of a marital break-up had seen him quit Mayday and take a break to mentally recover.

Who better to operate a wholesale business than a good administrator with a proven track record? He could bounce-back from domestic upheaval and we could all benefit.

Len liked the idea, so Garry and I funded the acquisition and gave Len a 20% share. Before long, he came to us with a bigger picture vision. Pet stores were traditionally "mum and pop" businesses and Len became annoyed at their "unreliability" and having to chase up tardy debtors. Having previously undertaken such a role, I appreciated how frustrating debt collection can be.

Len had a solution.

He recommended that we expand our vision and professionalise the industry by creating our own retail chain. That way, we could control the entire supply chain – from manufacturer/importer to customer.

Sounded like a smart and logical approach!

Key was to buy existing businesses in (or near) major shopping centres and pick up both the wholesale and retail margins.

It followed the fundamental fast-food outlet rule of *"location, location, location".*

All it needed was more money. So we funded acquisitions of four "plum" businesses as the start of the *"Li'l Friends"* chain and Len set about building the brand.

Certainly makes logical sense ... except for two things!

Firstly, under Warren Jones' oversight, Len was a great manager, but as the sole leader of a business given his head by two silent investors focussed on their own businesses – not so good.

Secondly, we had overlooked two very important factors – quality of staff and customer payment method.

The industry was one where most transactions were in cash (this was before the current credit card world) and without the owner's hand on the cash drawer, most stores had considerable "leakage" between customer and cash register that Len appeared unable to stem. We even "stock-spied" one store at night.

It got to the point that the expected margins had diminished to the extent that most sites we're battling just to break-even, let alone turn a profit.

By the time Garry and I decided that enough was enough and cut our losses, all goodwill (for which we had paid a premium to ensure prime locations) had evaporated and we were lucky to sell the stores at stock value.

While Garry and I had contributed only about $50,000 each initially, I had provided most of the loan funding for the expansion program. Though recovery of my loans was looking doubtful, it was secondary to my focus on my core business.

But back to disposal of the wholesale arm which was then the only profitable part of our pet business. We were naturally keen to exit this sorry situation quickly and stem the cash bleeding.

Only one willing buyer emerged – but he had no ready funds.

Shades of the barter days of ancient Rome, I accepted a Jensen Interceptor car (subsequently sold at a discount) and equity in a house as payment in order to recover some of my loan funds.

Then Len's termination arrangements needed to be addressed. Sympathetically, we let Len buy one of the smaller shops that he and his son could run and, with the benefit of hindsight, I foolishly funded the full purchase price on very flexible terms. The shop was less than successful, and the pain of character misjudgement has erased memory of the final settlement. What I do recall is that I had no wish to adversely affect what I perceived to be a fragile mental state by pursuing bankruptcy action which was likely to yield diddly-squat anyway.

So, we both moved on and despite him going on to create a successful pet food supply business, I never saw another cent from Len Hunt nor have I ever seen him again. Some people do have short memories!

My net losses ended up about $250,000. Silly me – should have stuck to the knitting that I controlled!

LESSONS:
1. DON'T SPREAD YOURSELF TOO THIN AND HAVE A VERY GOOD UNDERSTANDING OF THE NATURE OF THE BUSINESS AND ITS RISKS IF YOU DO NOT HAVE A HANDS-ON ROLE.
2. AS THE USUAL DISCLAIMER BY FUND MANAGERS STATES: PAST PERFORMANCE IS NO GUARANTEE OF FUTURE RESULTS … AND THAT EQUALLY APPLIES TO PEOPLE!

Timing is Everything | Peter J Snow OAM

A GOLDEN OPPORTUNITY

When I joined Australian Jaycees in 1970, it had 6,000 members in 250 chapters across Australia.

More than a decade later with its 50th Anniversary imminent, I successfully sought out and was appointed to the role of National Public Relations Officer.

What an opportunity to apply marketing flair and ideas – neither of which I have never had in short supply!

One of the Jaycee's hierarchy with a connection in Toyota's management had secured the donation of a gold coloured sedan – as a Golden Anniversary gift to the organisation.

It would be registered as JC-050 and was ultimately intended for use by the organisation's Secretariat Manager.

But what public relations exercise would optimise the image of both the organisation and the donor from such a generous gift?

Having been established in 1933, Perth Jaycees was the first chapter in Australia.

The 50th Anniversary National Convention was being held at Tweed Heads on the other side of the country with an opening ceremony at Seaworld on Queensland's Gold Coast.

Timing is Everything | Peter J Snow OAM

The answer was obvious.

Have a Jaycee team drive the car from the organisation's birthplace and delay the official handover to become part of the anniversary celebrations at Seaworld that was anticipated to attract more than a thousand delegates.

To optimise the promotion, have the Gold Toyota stop at 50 special events organised by Jaycee chapters along the way and call radio stations throughout Australia with progress reports.

Easy when you say it quickly - but look at the logistics involved.

To make it a media event, in days before mobile phones made communication so simple, a deal was done with Australia's Overseas Telecommunications Commission to provide a free live-to-air service for a donated ship-to-shore radio transceiver.

Sponsors were obtained for the bull bar, the transceiver and the special radio aerial. Fuel was donated by BP.

And to use it to raise money, link it to a sponsorship program at half a cent per kilometre – and don't require sponsors to commit to the whole distance of between six and seven thousand kms.

The incentive was to be free airfares for two and a week's holiday on the Gold Coast.

The Jaycees Community Foundation took the opportunity to promote its *"Whaleworld"* whaling station project by covering printing costs and sponsors decals on the car doors.

Timing is Everything | Peter J Snow OAM

Jaycees National President, Des Powell jumping for joy with JC-050 driving team Peter McKenzie, John Breeden and Allan McLean pre-Perth departure

As a public relations exercise, it was an absolute winner, achieving more than was expected or even hoped for.

The result was more than five hours of live-cross air-time on 40 radio stations across Australia, television coverage at stops along the way and articles in 55 newspapers. Radio crosses included Tasmania - even though the car did not travel there.

It also created public interest via civic receptions hosted by local government mayors and presidents during many of the 50 stops along the way. Some 30 new members joined the organisation.

Presentations were made to the Lord Mayors of each capital cities visited on a cross-country journey that took 16 days.

Timing is Everything | Peter J Snow OAM

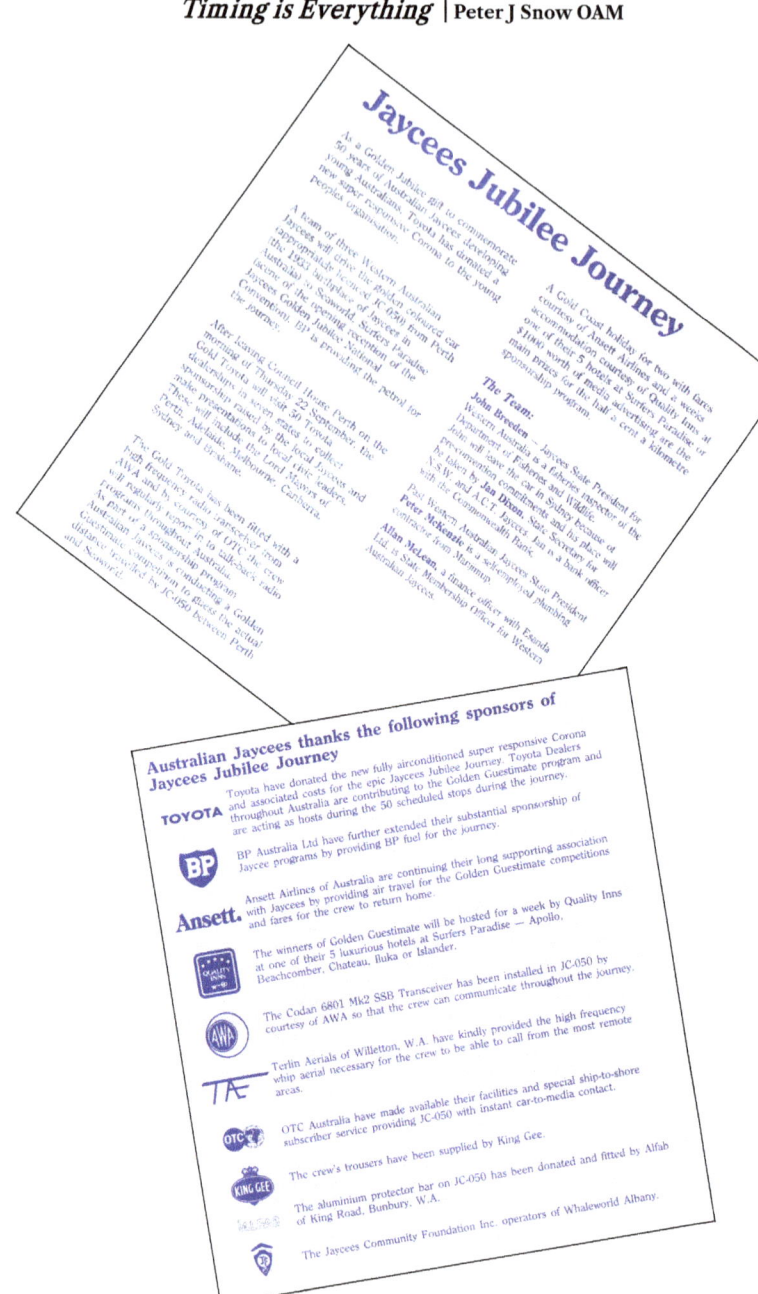

Jaycees Jubilee Journey

As a Golden Jubilee gift to commemorate 50 years of Australian Jaycees developing young Australians, Toyota has donated a new super responsive Corona to the Peoples Organisation.

A team of three Western Australian Jaycees will drive the Golden coloured car (appropriately named JC-050) from Perth to the 1983 National Convention of Jaycees in Australia's paradise of Seaworld, Surfers Paradise, for the opening ceremony of Jaycees Australian Golden Guestimate. Jaycees Jubilee National Convention. BP is providing the petrol for the journey.

After leaving Council House Perth on the morning of Thursday 22 September, the Gold Toyota is set off on its Golden dedication journey by the local Mayors and sponsorship as seen roles on 50 Toyota these presentations hosted by the local Jaycees Perth, will include, the Lord Mayors of Sydney, Adelaide, Melbourne, Canberra, Sydney and Brisbane.

The Gold Toyota has been fitted with a high frequency radio transceiver from AWA and by courtesy of OTC the crew will regularly report in to talkbacks radio programs throughout Australia.

As part of a membership Australian Guestimate, Jaycees is conducting a Golden distance competition to guess the actual distance travelled by JC-050 between Perth and Seaworld.

A Gold Coast holiday for two with fares courtesy of Ansett Airlines and a weeks accommodation courtesy of Quality Inns at one of their 5 hotels at Surfers Paradise, $1,000 worth of media advertising are the main prizes for the Jub's cent a kilometre sponsorship program.

The Team:

John Breeden — Jaycees State President for Western Australia — Jaycees State President for Department of Fisheries and Wildlife. John, will take the car to Sydney because of prior-commitments and in Sydney the car will be taken by **Ian Dixon**, State Secretary for NSW and ACT Jaycees. Ian is a bank officer with the Commonwealth Bank.

Peter McKenzie, Australian Jaycees State President contracted from Maranmoo, is a self-employed plumbing contractor.

Allan McLean, a finance officer with Esanda Ltd, is State Membership Officer for Western Australian Jaycees.

Australian Jaycees thanks the following sponsors of Jaycees Jubilee Journey

TOYOTA — Toyota have donated the new fully airconditioned super responsive Corona and associated costs for the epic Jaycees Jubilee Journey. Toyota Dealers throughout Australia are contributing to the Golden Guestimate program and are acting as hosts during the 50 scheduled stops during the journey.

BP — BP Australia Ltd have further extended their substantial sponsorship of Jaycee programs by providing BP fuel for the journey.

Ansett. — Ansett Airlines of Australia are continuing their long supporting association with Jaycees by providing air travel for the Golden Guestimate competitions and fares for the crew to return home.

QUALITY INNS — The winners of Golden Guestimate will be hosted for a week by Quality Inns at one of their 5 luxurious hotels at Surfers Paradise — Apollo, Beachcomber, Chateau, Iluka or Islander.

AWA — The Codan 6801 Mk2 SSB Transceiver has been installed in JC-050 by courtesy of AWA so that the crew can communicate throughout the journey.

TA — Terlin Aerials of Willetton, W.A. have kindly provided the high frequency whip aerial necessary for the crew to be able to call from the most remote areas.

OTC — OTC Australia have made available their facilities and special ship-to-shore subscriber service providing JC-050 with instant car-to-media contact.

KING GEE — The crew's trousers have been supplied by King Gee.

ALFAB — The aluminium protector bar on JC-050 has been donated and fitted by Alfab of King Road, Bunbury, W.A.

JCF — The Jaycees Community Foundation Inc. operators of Whaleworld Albany.

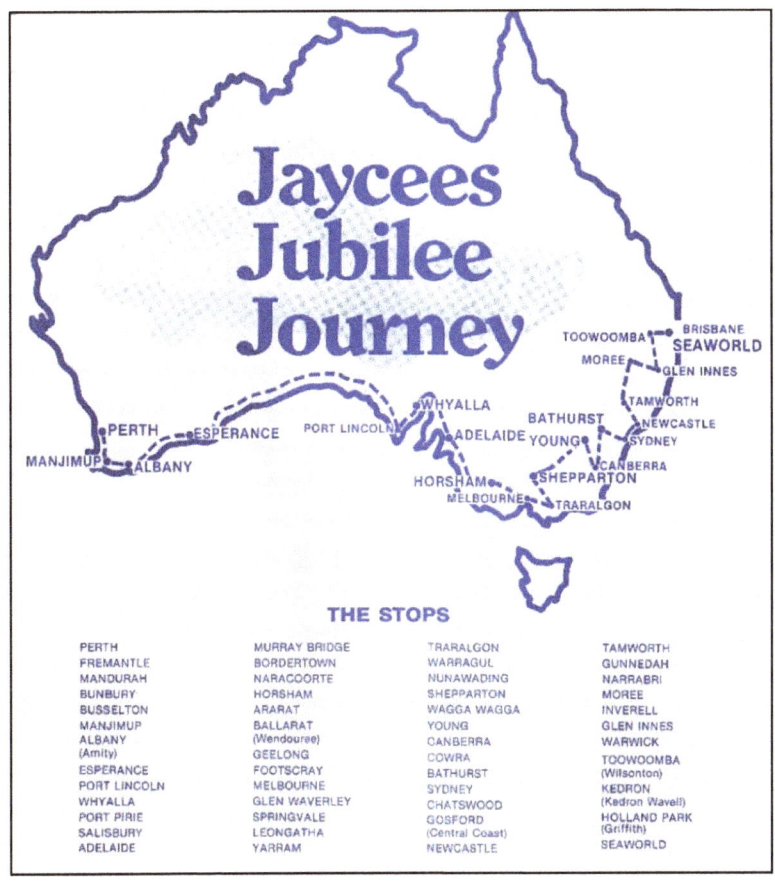

The *Jaycees Jubilee Journey* was one part of an extensive public relations program that included an Australia Post stamp issue, branding on millions of Coles shopping bags, a promotional film and television and radio commercials.

Australia's program was recognised with both Asia-Pacific and JCI World Awards for *Best National Public Relations Program.*

Where there's a Will ... there's a Way

Our Foundation was looking for a benefactor to contribute up to $50,000 towards the cost of a proposed exhibit at Whaleworld – Australia's last whaling station – a struggling heritage museum.

One fundraiser was a small booklet called the World of Whales we had commissioned Sally Foy, an English natural history writer to produce. A little later, Sally approached me with a problem. She and geologist Cliff Morris - in collaboration with highly-regarded nature photographers Bert and Babs Wells, had completed work on a coffee table book of unique wildlife and scenery in Western Australia's Pilbara. Two mining companies committed to partially underwriting the publication had pulled out - leaving the project in limbo.

Having seen the compendium of remarkable animal images, not publishing it would be an absolute tragedy.

In mentally addressing potential benefactors with connections to the mining industry, the name Danny Hill came to mind. I had previously had some dealings with the hard-nosed mining entrepreneur who controlled several mining companies.

Knowing there was no way he would gift $50,000 to a whaling station museum at the opposite end of the state, I coaxed him to a lunch and allowed him to view the quality images before asking him for $44,000 to cover the production cost of 5,000 copies.

Based on us donating (on his behalf) one book to every school library in the state and swayed by the remarkable photos and possibly influenced by the second bottle of wine, he (or at least his mining companies) agreed to my request.

The launch of The Wild Pilbara was held at the Ministry for Education with the acting Minister for Education, Andrew Mensaros MLA, accepting the 1,000 donated books on behalf of the state education system.

ABOVE RIGHT: Minister Andrew Mensaros MLA (centre) with donor Mr Danny Hill (right), the Authors and Jaycees Community Foundation Board Members

What happened to the other 4,000 copies? Well, the Foundation sold them and raised the $50,000 we had originally sought.

Where there's a will ... there's a way!

Timing is Everything | Peter J Snow OAM

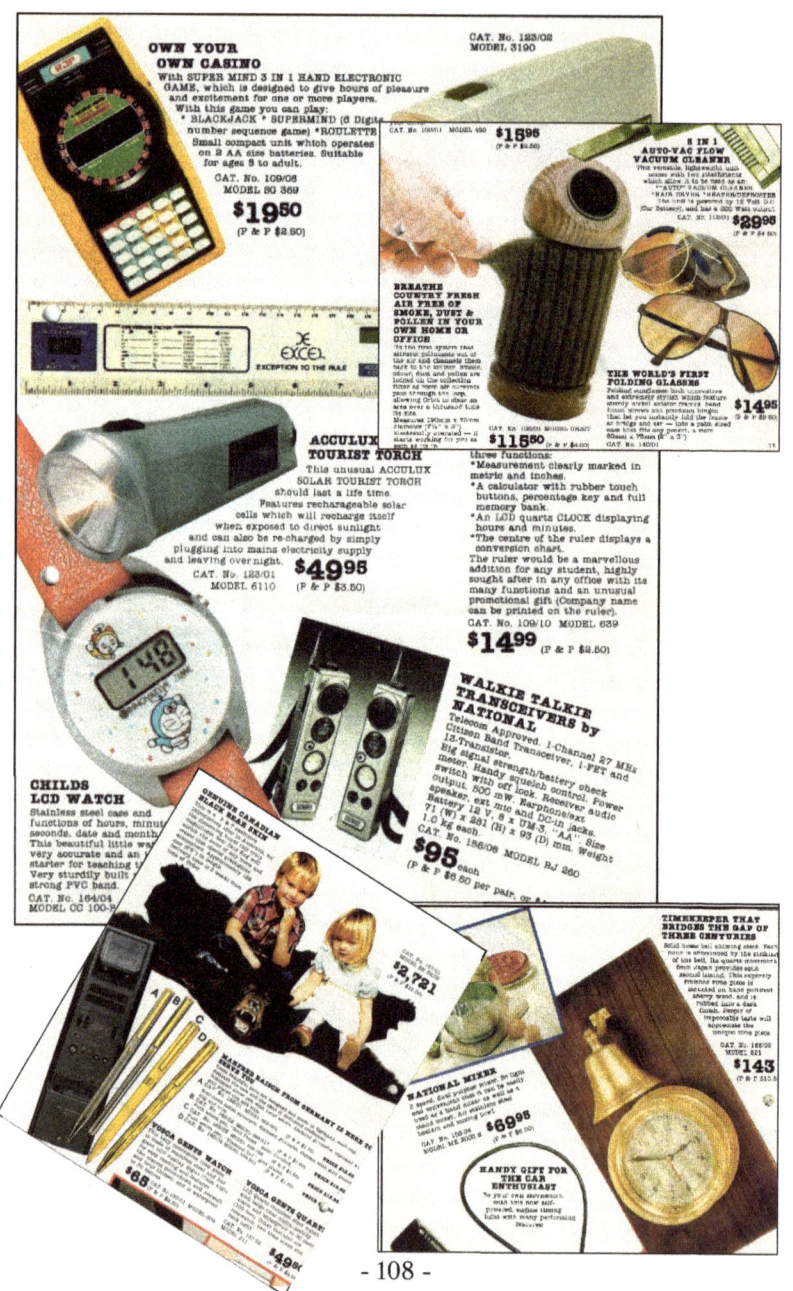

Timing is Everything | Peter J Snow OAM

IT TURNED INTO A STAMPEDE!

Don Loxton (one of original Management Consortiums backers and later a partner in our Diamond Hire business) requested we chat with a former Mayday Hire colleague. I remembered Tony Menikides as a Welsh giant of a man. A rigger of scaffolding by day, Tony claimed to have sold 4,000 wrist watches through verbose text advertisements on the inside cover of the Sunday paper.

He wanted to upscale this side hustle and test a mail-order catalogue. As the owner of *The Paper Tigers* word-processing bureau at the time, I saw this as a possible opportunity to deploy some unused staff time in processing and packaging orders.

We formed *Australian Mailorder Co. Pty Ltd* and registered *P & T Direct Marketing Co.* as its trading business name. Tony was Managing Director and Don and I were financiers and Directors.

Tony set to locating samples of a wide range of merchandise for a new 44-page mail order test catalogue.

With a trial run of 50,000 copies, the test catalogue only just broke-even – not even recovering overheads or Tony's salary.

Should we punt on a roll-out and expansion of that business?

Timing is Everything | Peter J Snow OAM

No. What tipped the scales was a cease-and-desist letter from lawyers representing a brand of high-end sunglasses.

The manufacturer's sample for the catalogue happened to be a branded sample and that had appeared in the catalogue. The problem was our price was less than a tenth of the same (but branded) version. Understandably, the owners of the brand name were more than a little miffed.

Thus, we abandoned thoughts of pouring more funds into what could be a bottomless pit and sent Tony in search of alternatives.

The catalogue had included a range of quality Manfred Raisch pens from Germany. Somehow, master salesman Tony managed to obtain an order from the Blind Association for 50,000 ball-point pens. These were indented directly from the German manufacturer to the charity's office for its annual tele-sales fund-raising campaign – donate $20 and receive a "free" pen.

At a margin of $2 each we recovered our operating losses (plus some). Wish we could do that every day!

What next? Tony came up with the idea of stamp collections.

At the time, Australia Post distributed 600,000 copies of Stamp News – a free monthly newsletter of interest to the nation's philatelists.

His was a simple idea. Insert a promotional brochure for a stamp-related product in Stamp News (as it was a far cheaper alternative to traditional mailing campaigns). But what product?

With the 250th Anniversary of Lloyd's of London (the insurance underwriters) imminent, an artist designed a mock-up album commemorating the event and a sales brochure. At $149, it was to contain mint sets of commemorative stamps and a first day cover from 17 Commonwealth countries. According to Tony's stamp research, philatelists rank stamps from Commonwealth countries second only to Australian stamps.

It was an extraordinary success. We had 1,000 prepaid orders and nearly $150,000 in our bank before we had actually produced a finished product – probably not something you would be permitted to do today.

We moved on to bigger things with the World Communications Year Collection containing 375 stamps from 130 countries and went public - forming *International Philatelic Corporation Ltd.*

IPC was the 13th company listed on Perth Stock Exchange's new Second Board for small companies.

Tony was Managing Director and my company was retained to provide my services as a marketing and corporate consultant.

Timing is Everything | Peter J Snow OAM

In 1983, when Australia created history by becoming the first non-USA winner of the America's Cup's in 132 years, it meant defending the Cup in Perth in 1987.

What a great opportunity to produce the America's Cup in Stamps. With Australia Post unlikely to allow exploitation of its stamps for commercial gain, which country should we approach?

As negotiator of all the contracts and licensing deals, I accompanied Tony to the Solomon Islands and we secured the rights to produce the island Commonwealth country's America's Cup stamps. As we were landing, the pilot warned: "*Welcome to Honiara, I hope you have had your typhoid and malaria shots*". We had had neither. It was like stepping into a scene from Mutiny on the Bounty – except for the sophisticated Japanese telephone system – courtesy of a European overseas aid grant aimed at supporting European manufacturers – ironically no European company tendered.

Normally half-day negotiations stretched to nearly three days and we were to meet both the Minister and Prime Minister for a licence that ultimately delivered the island nation project royalties that exceeded their usual annual philatelic revenue.

With appropriate introductions, I was able to finalise licencing arrangements with syndicates representing Australia, NZ and USA (Dennis Conner). What followed were distribution deals for collector album and piece-a-week programs with Coles New World Supermarkets (Australia) and Woolworths (NZ).

A tele-sales campaign with TVNZ International, New Zealand's state television network was also agreed.

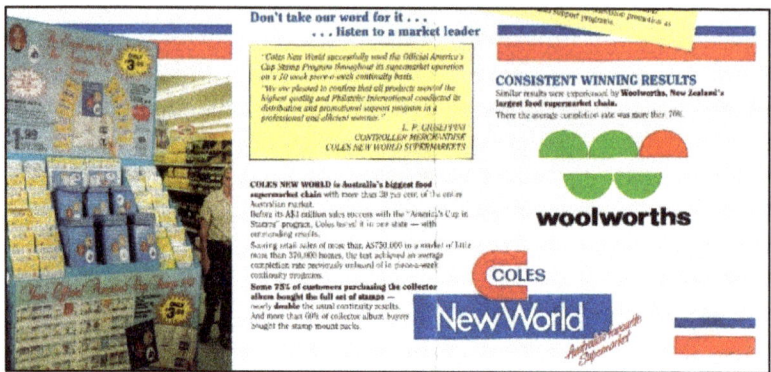

The retail sales were based on the traditional piece-a-week crockery programs. It started with a value-for-money collector album at only $3.99 followed by 10 weeks with packets of 5 stamps at $1.99 so that in the end, customers would have the whole set of 50 stamps – every past winner and all contenders for the 1987 cup. The 250,000 Album production run was Australia's largest book printing run to that time.

Dennis Conner is arguably the best-known America's Cup skipper. He recorded two TV commercials aimed primarily at the US market. These were tested in California, Western Australia and Tasmania as a precursor to advertising campaigns to be based on revenue-sharing arrangements.

That entailed the TV stations receiving a percentage of revenue rather than fixed rate advertising fees – a great marketing method where all parties share risk and reward. For us it meant no sales – no advertising costs (apart from the TV commercials).

Monitoring of the test commercials showed that California and Western Australia were likely to be successful, Tasmania not so.

Luck followed. Ted Turner (owner of CNN and former Cup skipper), with whom I had been attempting to meet for more than a year, saw the test commercials running in California and demanded that the promotion be run on all 17 of his affiliate stations. Copies of the 17 master tapes were hand-carried to the USA to guarantee timely arrival and screening.

At its peak, a 200-staff answering service in Utah was taking orders and I was receiving hourly reports in Perth on responses to the TV spots. With the 12-14 hour time difference, we realised that many viewers must be recording races in Australia and then ordering while watching replays when they woke up - rather than during live telecasts. This distorted data measurement.

In six weeks, USA TV sales reached $1 million out of the $6 million global sales the program achieved.

Orders from a single screening of a Dennis Conner commercial created a record for direct sales on U.S. television's sports channel ESPN. Dennis's royalties far exceeded his expectations and resulted in the hint of a job offer with him in San Diego – which I thought about briefly ... but chose to ignore.

Flushed with success and after securing licensing deals with Disney and Major League Baseball in the USA, IPC established an office in Salt Lake City, Utah.

The public company Board decided to appoint a "business" CEO and Tony was relegated to General Manager - Marketing.

The Australian CEO sent to Utah to "manage" IPC's North American operations became enamoured with marketing rather than managing. In the absence of advance orders to underwrite risk, and against the Board's specific direction, he ran up big commitments for display materials. As a result, I was despatched to Utah to "tidy up" a less than satisfactory situation.

In a scenario akin to Wesfarmers attempt to infuse the Bunnings hardware concept into British culture, IPC was to suffer a similar fate in the USA with its piece-a-week stamp programs despite the strength of the branded products it had – albeit with a much smaller loss.

However, the disaster in the USA, coupled with minimal residual funds, spooked the major shareholders into some corporate house-keeping and they off-loaded their interests in the listed corporate shell to investors who had a new direction in mind.

Exciting as it had been - the great Stampede was over!

Ironically, IPC still exists today – but under its replacement name - International Equities Corporation Ltd (ASX: IEQ) and is now operating in the hospitality and property development areas – a far cry from its original purpose.

LESSONS:
1. COMPLETE ALL THE "WHAT IF'S" AS PART OF YOUR ORIGINAL ASSESSMENT OF A PROJECT AND PLAN ACCORDINGLY.
2. MAKE SURE YOU HAVE CONTINGENCY PLAN B … AND PLAN C … IF PLAN A DOES NOT FLY.
3. BE FLEXIBLE AND PIVOT IF YOU NEED TO.
4. HORSES FOR COURSES – SELECT THE RIGHT PEOPLE THAT ARE THE BEST AVAILABLE IN THEIR RESPECTIVE FIELDS (POACH THEM IF NECESSARY) – BUT THEN DON'T ASSIGN THEM TO OTHER SKILL AREAS.
5. CONSIDER HOW YOU WILL ADDRESS A PROBLEM IF IT IS REMOTE FROM YOUR LOCATION AND IS NOT CONVENIENTLY ACCESSIBLE.

Timing is Everything | Peter J Snow OAM

RIGHT PLACE – RIGHT TIME !

I was in New York meeting with Inter-Governmental Philatelic Corporation to negotiate the purchase of stamps for one of International Philatelic's stamp collections when I noted that they represented the Republic of Palau. It is an archipelago of more than 500 islands in the Micronesia region of the Western Pacific Ocean.

The reason for my interest was that I had seen a set of Palau stamps that featured whale paintings and enquired about the artist.

Puzzled by my question, they revealed that they had commissioned local artist Richard Ellis to design the Palau stamps and would happily introduce me – which they did.

This led to an amazing chain of events that very much relates to the sub-title of this book.

I was to learn that he was an internationally renowned artist and author and among his many commissions, was a 29 m (94 foot) blue whale suspended in the Hall of Ocean Life at the American Museum of Natural History in New York.

It is the most amazing marine exhibit you will ever see.

Intending to ask him about his Palau whale stamps, I arranged a dinner with Richard during which I proudly showed him the award submission on the Jaycees Community Foundation's whaling station project.

Timing is Everything | Peter J Snow OAM

The submission had resulted in a world award at the JCI World Congress in Montreal the previous week for the Best Joint Work by a Group of Jaycees.

During the dinner, Richard mentioned that he was soon to take delivery of his collection of 106 original marine mammal paintings after completion of a two-year tour of the Americas arranged by the Smithsonian Institution.

This confronted him with a dilemma. His apartment was too small to take his large collection - all framed and in reinforced travelling exhibition cases.

Recognising an opportunity, I enquired as to how much he would want for the collection if he was prepared to part with it?

When learning it would be destined for a whaling museum on the other side of the world, Richard nominated US$25,000.

With a quick mental calculation of the unit price of 106 original marine mammal acrylic paintings as making this the deal of the year, I sought a three-month option. This would allow me time to find a benefactor on my return to Western Australia to fund the purchase.

At the time, the Foundation was conducting a pilot program for the Australian Government's Community Employment Program for long-term unemployed. The $565,000 grant funded the employment of 56 people for six months.

One was John Leach, a senior marketing executive.

Between us, we put together a "pitch" book aimed at local entrepreneur Kevin Parry, whom I had identified as a potential benefactor.

He had sponsored Parry Field – the state's main baseball field and was also a patron of Subiaco Football Club - confirming him as a real prospect.

As fate has a way of intervening, I happened to be visiting my mother and mentioned our plan to approach Mr Parry. *"Well, you had better hurry"* was her reaction. *"He is leaving tomorrow for a six-week overseas trip".*

This information had come from Parry's neighbour who regularly played Bridge with my dear mother.

In fear of losing our prime target, I implored John to deliver our pitch book to Parry – even if it meant handing it to him as he was boarding an aircraft. He was too late. Parry was gone.

Second choice was Parry's public relations section which rebuffed the approach with a *"Kevin would not be interested".*

The option clock was ticking. With revamped submissions, unsuccessful approaches were made to other entrepreneurs – Alan Bond, Robert Holmes A'Court and even Ansett Airlines (Australia's second largest airline).

Time was running out. With the option lapse looming and Parry now back in town, I suggested John revisit the prospect of Parry.

Timing is Everything | Peter J Snow OAM

Persistence paid, Kevin Parry, through one of his companies - NBN Newcastle (a television broadcaster on Australia's east coast) bought and donated the world's largest collection of original marine mammal paintings. These are now proudly displayed in the Parry Gallery at Albany's Historic Whaling Station. We even prevailed on Qantas to assist and they, in conjunction with an American affiliate, freighted the collection to Perth at no charge.

ABOVE: Foundation benefactor Kevin Parry with Richard Ellis at the Perth handover of the Richard Ellis Collection

Timing is Everything | Peter J Snow OAM

ABOVE: A Richard Ellis Walrus painting

ABOVE: The Richard Ellis Display

LESSONS:

1. IF AT FIRST YOU DON'T SUCCEED, THERE IS NOTHING LOST IN HAVING A SECOND ATTEMPT - EXCEPT TIME.
2. ALWAYS TRY TO PRESENT TO THE DECISION-MAKER.
3. IDENTIFY WHY A DEAL WOULD APPEAL TO A BACKER OR BACKERS AND PRIORITISE THEM.
4. IF SEEKING MONEY, PRODUCE A PROFESSIONAL PITCH BOOK. ONE-OFF PHOTOBOOKS ARE RELATIVELY CHEAP TO PRODUCE.

POSTSCRIPT 1: Richard Ellis had been diving with white pointer sharks at Port Lincoln in South Australia on commission for National Geographic. We managed to have him detour to Perth for the official handover of his collection after which he presented me with a gift. It was the printer's proof of his Year of the Ocean poster of Whales of American Waters commissioned by the President of the United States. Thinking it would be great for him to do a similar poster of Whales of Australian Waters, I queried the commission from the President.

It was US$25,000!!

So, did we get a bargain? A collection of 106 original paintings for the cost of a single poster!

POSTSCRIPT 2: During dinner with Richard, he backgrounded me on his various commissions with the likes of Audubon Magazine and National Geographic and his writings on marine animals.
[He published over 30 books including authoritative works – The Book of Whales and The Book of Sharks].

As an inaugural subscriber to Dick Smith's Australian Geographic, I recalled mention of a future article on whales and thought it was worth at least an enquiry. Being in my hotel's restaurant, I suggested we return to my room and make a call to Australian Geographic on an off-chance. You can be cheeky!

Having said *"This is Peter Snow calling from New York to speak to Mr Smith,"* amazingly I was put straight through to the man himself. It resulted in an invitation to visit Dick at his Sydney office in Terrey Hills on my way back to Perth. I am pleased to report that it resulted in Richard's 21-page article, the cover picture and an accompanying poster in Australian Geographic. Glad we could indirectly repay Richard's collection generosity.

POSTSCRIPT 3: Many years later, as parts of the Parry empire encountered some difficulties, the Liquidator of NBN Newcastle requested a return of the Richard Ellis Collection that had been "lent" to the Foundation.

After advising them of the history of the "donation" nothing more was heard from the Liquidators and the Richard Ellis Collection remains one of Albany's Historic Whaling Station's key exhibits.

Timing is Everything | Peter J Snow OAM

FROM "RENT-A-COW" TO A WORLD FOOD SOLUTION

Nearly 50 years ago I had a brief encounter with the world of genetics as Secretary of company involved in pure-bred cattle.

Unlike today's sophisticated invitro-fertilisation programs that satisfy human reproduction desires, back then it was about a cattle breeding program we called our "Rent-a-cow" program.

This was simply a clever way to accelerate the herd growth of pure-bred cattle on an exponential basis.

The nature of the process was easy to understand and appealed to medical professionals who became the primary investor market. The Maher Group (referred to in an earlier tale) had acquired a quality rural property of nearly eight thousand hectares (or 19,500 acres) known as "Woodyarup" at Broomehill, some 300 kilometres south of Perth, Western Australia.

What was believed to be the state's first commercial ovum transplant centre for cattle was constructed and proceeded to produce what reportedly became the largest herd of pure-bred Charolais and Simmental cattle in the southern hemisphere.

There was no magic. It involved super-ovulation treatment and invitro-fertilisation of the pure-breds, harvesting the fertilised ova and transplanting them into "surrogate" (but much cheaper) host cows. An investor would be guaranteed a minimum of two live pure-bred calves out of eight fertilised transplanted ova under a type of all-inclusive "lease" arrangement.

The all-inclusive fee was $36,500 for Charolais or $42,000 for Simmental. While the prices may shock you, there was a reasonable commercial incentive ... if you were considered to be carrying on a business as a pure-bred cattle breeder a tax deduction for the full investment was possible. Any calves were brought to account as stock on hand at $2 each instead of market value meaning you could "defer" the "profit" to another day.

Charolais originated from a region of France of the same name. They are raised for meat and may be crossed with other breeds including Angus and Hereford cattle and are among the heaviest of cattle breeds. Bulls weigh from 1,000 to 1,650 kg (2,200 to 3,600 lb), and cows from 700 to 1,200 kg (1,500 to 2,600 lb). The coat ranges from white to cream-coloured and the nose is uniformly pink. Recent prices for Bulls have ranged from $8,000 to $90,000 with a record at $265,000.

Simmental originated from the valley of the same name on the Simme River in the Swiss canton of Berne. The breed is typically reddish in colour with white markings and has historically been used for dairy and beef. It is renowned for rapid growth with more combined weaning gain (growth) and milk yield than any other breed. A recent price check on Simmental bulls ranged from $10,000 to a record $160,000.

So, depending on how many calves (particularly bulls) out of the eight ova transplanted - it was potentially a good investment. Amazingly, the ova transplanting and surrogacy process bears remarkable similarity to the process used by humans today.

Moving forward 30 years and towards the end of my career as CEO of a boutique venture capital firm, the Evandale House Group encountered a clever molecular biologist and geneticist by the name of Dr Peter Kay.

Before retirement as Head of the University of Western Australia's Molecular Pathology Laboratory he had a 22-year career in its Department of Pathology. The author or co-author of more than 90 peer reviewed scientific papers, he was a clever man with an idea ... a very clever idea.

His many years of genetic research had led him to look at the processes behind Hybrid Vigour. For those unfamiliar with this term, here is a very simple explanation.

Farmers, breeders and agriculturists have crossed unrelated strains of plants and different breeds of animals for thousands of years in order to generate superior offspring.

Sometimes the offspring of unrelated parents are bigger, healthier, grow quicker and are more fertile than either of their parents. Offspring with these qualities are said to exhibit Hybrid Vigour.

Well over a hundred years ago, the evolutionary biologist Charles Darwin was the first to recognize that Hybrid Vigour had played an important role in the process of natural evolution.

He was the first to apply scientific principles towards understanding the biology of this very important evolutionary tool.

Timing is Everything | Peter J Snow OAM

It is known that through cross-breeding the right parent animals you can produce offspring that are bigger, stronger or faster than each of the parents. In the case of food there is the possibility of better quality and quantity of cereal crops and other plants.

From a technical perspective, Peter Kay's experimentation showed that when two parent lines were cross-bred, a new protein could be developed in the offspring that wasn't in the DNA of either parent and so therefore could not be inherited.

He started developing technology that enabled identification of the genes that drive Hybrid Vigour by looking at the molecular genetic mechanisms. Then, having identified the relevant genes, with minimal genetic changes required within them, they could be genetically "fixed" to develop consistent superior food crops.

What it meant was that rather than taking years and years to evolve naturally as farmers already did to maximise yield, the technology could allow the process to be sped up to make crops that were more productive, healthier, stronger and much easier to breed. The new "formula" would allow superior qualities to pass from offspring to offspring enabling the reproduction of "super" seeds year on year.

Conversely, many human health complaints that arise through Hybrid Debility could be addressed in the same way.

Eureka! A global solution to the world's food and many health problems!

Below are the potential applications:

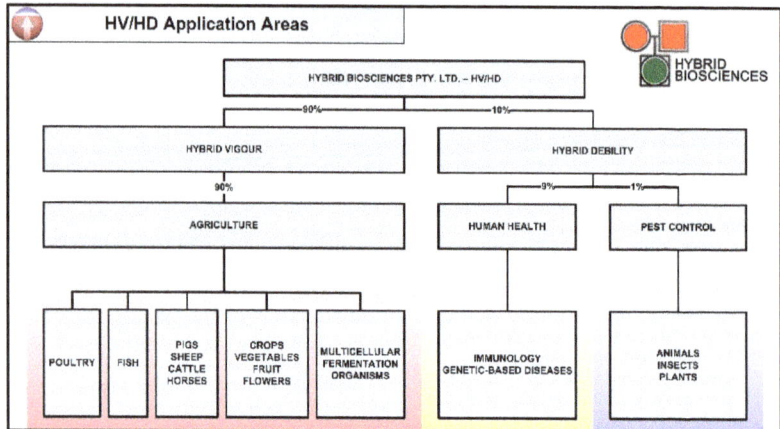

Hybrid Biosciences Pty Ltd was formed to take this world-changing technology to the market. With my retirement, Bruce Gallash undertook conduct and funding of this exciting project. The first step was to protect the technology through patents.

An International Patent Application 2006274514 was granted in Australia for a: *"Method of Identifying Genes which Promote Hybrid Vigour and Hybrid Debility and uses thereof."*

A second International Patent Application PCT/AU2006/001065 was lodged for: *"Identification of Genes and their Products which Promote Hybrid Vigour and Hybrid Debility and uses thereof."*
An extract from the Second Patent Application reads:
'The invention relates to a method of identifying candidate genes and the proteins encoded by them that are useful in the inducement of hybrid vigour, hybrid debility and/or diagnosis, prognosis and treatment of disease.

In particular, the present invention relates to a method of identifying factors leading to hybrid vigour or hybrid debility comprising identifying the presence or absence of multiple species of mRNA or protein encoded by alleles of a candidate gene, wherein the presence of multiple species of mRNA or protein is indicative of hybrid vigour or hybrid debility".

Now for the non-technical like me, that all sounds interesting but converting this to practical reality is an entirely different kettle of fish.

A global patent application process was commenced with patents granted in Singapore, New Zealand and South Africa. Applications were made in the European Union, USA, Canada, Republic of Korea, Israel, India, Japan, Hong Kong and China.

But patents and renewals thereof demand significant funding and while the outcome of the application of the technology should be world changing, there was a major obstacle.

While knowing its intended outcomes, understanding the technology was an issue. I profess that to this day, I never fully understood how it worked. But, as it transpired, I was not on my own. Potential backers approached generally referred Bruce to their "Adviser". Rather than admit that they did not understand the technology and how it worked, the "Advisers" cast doubt on it - resulting in a "thank you - but no thank you" response.

Rice was seen as a big opportunity. Research identified China National Hybrid Rice Research and Development Center based in Mapoling, Changsha, in China's Hunan Province as a potential "partner". By its very name, they knew about Hybrid Vigour.

Its Director-General, Professor Yuan Longping was recognised internationally as the "Father of Hybrid Rice" and considered to be a Chinese National Treasure with a string of awards including the World Food Prize. So, Hybrid Biosciences granted Professor Yuan's Research Center a licence with the objective of proving up the technology with trials that would dispel the scepticism.

Language difficulties and the technical nature of the technology prevented a full understanding of progress, but nothing came of the arrangement so we will never know if trials were actually undertaken or the license was simply taken up to "bury" it to prevent the technology being used by potential competitors.

To my knowledge, the people that really understood it could be counted on fingers of one hand and even, after recently coming across a spare copy of the relevant papers and patent and sending it to a professor in the field of genetics, he admitted that he didn't. So, I don't feel too bad about my lack of understanding.

What has happened since? The various patents have lapsed and what could have been a world saviour in food and health remains unexploited.

LESSONS:
1. IF YOU DON'T UNDERSTAND HOW SOMETHING WORKS THEN TRY TO FIND SOMEONE WHO CAN EXPLAIN IT TO YOU IN NON-TECHNICAL TERMS.
2. ENSURE LICENCES HAVE PERFORMANCE AND LAPSE CLAUSES. IF THAT IS NOT POSSIBLE MOVE ON.
3. CONSIDER FIRST MOVER ADVANTAGE AGAINST PROTECTION VIA THE LEGAL SYSTEM. ASSESS COSTS AND ONGOING FEES BEFORE COMMITTING.

Timing is Everything | Peter J Snow OAM

A WHALE OF A TALE!

In 1979 I was working out of a hotel room on the other side of Australia on Queensland's Gold Coast wrapping up the Perth corporate documentation for the Maher group when, by another stroke of luck, I encountered an old client.

In quest of a tomato juice, I had been walking through a nearly deserted bar in my hotel's lobby at about 4.00 pm when I noticed a hand waving at me from a small group in one corner.

It was Colin Green from Harvey Beef, Western Australia's biggest beef exporters - with whom I had concluded a single deal some four years earlier.

After exchanging pleasantries, I declined his invitation to join the group and also a dinner invitation, as I expected to be working through the night to complete my assignment so that I could return to Perth the next morning.

Tomato juice in hand, I ventured back to my room and set about finalising my documentation when I was disturbed by the ring of my room phone at about 9.00 pm.

It was Colin with: *"This is silly, you have to eat!"* Close to the completion of my work, I agreed to join him for dinner in the hotel restaurant. Interspersed with an assortment of beverages, I learnt that since our last meeting years before, the Green's family company had completed a takeover of the publicly-listed Cheynes Beach Whaling Company Ltd.

They had held shares for many years and were aware that it had some under-valued investments separate to the whaling station.

After their on-market clean-up of minorities, they had privatised the company and closed its whaling operations.

Recalling media coverage a few months earlier that the closure had been a big commercial blow to Albany with the company's 106 workers now out of work, I queried the reasons and the fate of the industrial complex 400km south of Perth. Remember, this was just a few months after Australia's last whaling operation ceased on 21 November 1978.

After explaining that viability, shrinking markets, alternative products, run-down equipment, doubt over whale quotas and renewal of the annual noxious industry licence was the reason (rather than the very public pressure from conservationists), Colin addressed the rest of my question.

They had salvaged any equipment that could be used in Greens' abattoir at Harvey and auctioned off whatever was left ... except, he had a problem with three ships – well two, actually.

Apparently, the successful tenderer for the three whaling ships had a clause in the contract that allowed recission if he could not get heavy duty lifting gear onto the town jetty where they were moored. The plan had been to cut the ships up at the jetty and load the scrap metal onto trucks .... but ... barnacles had eaten the jetty pylons - making it unsafe. Unable to proceed, the three vessels had been returned to Colin.

Timing is Everything | Peter J Snow OAM

He went on to explain that he had "promised" one to Senator Ken Wriedt for the Hobart Maritime Museum.

Fascinated by this ship-trading, I queried the value of the tender. $6,000 each was the answer. On learning that this would deliver a 45m, 530-ton ship, I immediately offered to buy one *"on condition that it is delivered to the Swan River"*.

My spur of the moment thought bubble was to find a benefactor to donate the required $6,000 to The Jaycees Community Foundation that I then chaired, locate an accessible mooring site in the Swan River, assign an "old salt" to caretaking duties and charge $2 per head for onboard access.

I reasoned that most people in Perth had never seen a whale-chaser let alone had the opportunity to go aboard one. This could raise at least $50,000 annually for our charity.

Astounded by the imaginative idea, Colin volunteered to donate one to what seemed to him to be a worthy cause.

With somewhat heavy heads after more beverages than desirable, we both rang our respective right-hand people to convey follow up arrangements for this exceptional gift.

On my return to Perth, and with a mooring arranged near a yacht club at East Fremantle, I fielded a call from Peter McGrath, Greens' finance director - wanting to meet me.

I greeted him in my City office with a draft of the press release about our plans for the intended maritime gift.

Timing is Everything | Peter J Snow OAM

"Small problem he explained. It is going to cost about $30,000 to fuel and crew it to Perth - but that's not all. Because of its poor condition and risk of sinking in transit and becoming a maritime hazard, a million-dollar insurance bond is required - so we don't want to proceed."

Not hiding my disappointment, I responded with *"Our team will be devastated"* to which he replied: *"What about the whaling station?"*

With $50,000 annual income mentally evaporating I repeated: *"What about the whaling station?"*

"Do you want that?" was the reply.

"Why not?" was mine – not thinking what that might involve.

And that is how Australia's last whaling station, complete with six whaler's cottages, two whaling ships, 300 bent harpoons and what remained of the processing plant and equipment was gifted to The Jaycees Community Foundation Inc.

It took nearly two years of red tape before the gift was consummated. The site was rezoned to "Museum and Youth Camp" and the annual noxious industry licence converted to a 10-year "peppercorn" lease with an 11-year option over the 20-hectare (50 acre) site on the shores of the magnificent King George Sound.

The lease was granted to the Greens on 12 December 1980. The gift was formalised three days later.

Timing is Everything | Peter J Snow OAM

On Boxing Day, 26 December 1980, *"Whaleworld"* museum opened for business.

The mammoth task to convert a derelict industrial site into a viable heritage attraction had begun.

Timing is Everything | Peter J Snow OAM

A management partnership was agreed with the whaling company's former pilot, John Bell and his wife - and operated until John's tragic death in an aircraft accident 16 years later.

First issue to address was the relocation of the two whale-chasers to put an end to the $500 a month mooring fees at Albany's Town Jetty.

The Cheynes III, was scuttled as a diving practise wreck - but only after its unique triple expansion steam engine had been salvaged to become a working exhibit. It was meticulously restored by marine engineer volunteers from Fremantle.

PICTURE CREDIT: STEVE STRIKE

Receiving no tenders to relocate the better condition Cheynes IV to the site, John Bell, with bulldozers and ingenuity, berthed Australia's last whale-chaser alongside the whale oil tanks.

Next, the Foundation pioneered the Community Employment Program in Western Australia obtaining a grant of $565,000.

This provided 6-months work for 56 long-term unemployed.

A new entrance complex was built and derelict buildings and equipment restored.

Few knew that cost over-runs meant that the Foundation Board personally guaranteed the first $50,000 of a $180,000 loan - at a 24% (yes, 24%) interest rate. It was repaid two years early.

Timing is Everything | Peter J Snow OAM

Lotterywest grants funded construction of the Axel Christensen Dock and the audio re-enactment of a whale-chase on the Cheynes IV.

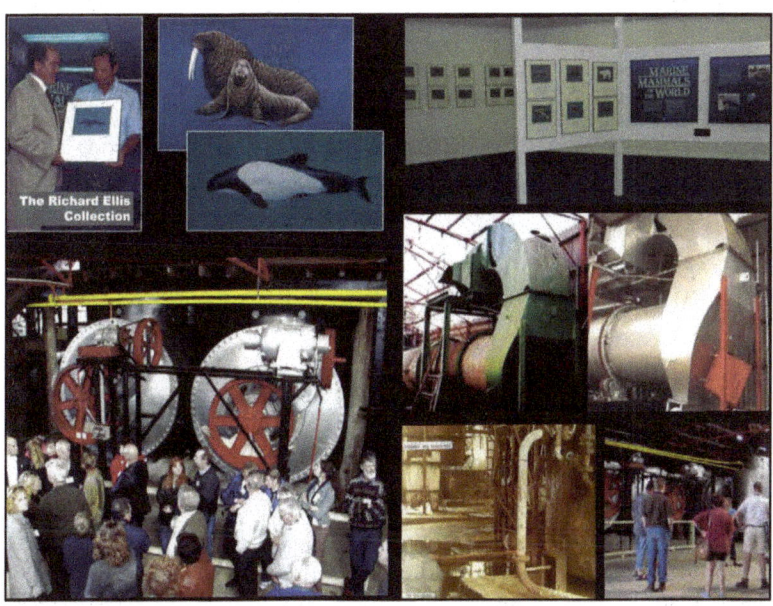

The late Kevin Parry donated the world's largest collection of 106 marine mammal paintings by international marine artist Richard Ellis and Qantas sponsored freight to Australia. Further audio re-enactments have brought the processing factory to life.

A collection of 56 photos of the last eight years of whaling was acquired from the Albany Advertiser's photographer Ed Smidt and are now displayed in the station's Colin Green Gallery. Its conversion from a derelict storage shed to a two-level gallery was partly funded by a Heritage grant and the Green Family.

The site boasts the state's largest whale skeleton display - and further grant funding has seen three whale oil tanks converted into unique theatres.

One delivers an 8-minute history of Australian whaling. Another covers the interaction between sharks and the whalers and the third presents the world's first 3D animated whale film which was proudly created in Perth.

The fourth tank details the roles, and pays tribute to, the many whaling station workers for whom the sudden closure and loss of 106 jobs was a bitter pill.

Two whale-themed playgrounds were developed for children of all ages.

Timing is Everything | Peter J Snow OAM

All these exhibits had trebled site visitation time to more than three hours but a half day at a whaling museum was less than appealing on tour brochures. How could we optimise visitor numbers? The plan was to appoint a CEO to look at the long-term of "what could be".

Sciona Browne was Executive Director at The Evandale House Group (of which I was CEO at the time) and was the Foundation's part-time Executive Officer – partly subsidised by EHG. As the then non-executive Chairman of the Foundation this was a very convenient way to keep tabs on the goings on while maintaining my corporate obligations to The Evandale House Group's diverse project portfolio.

At this point, I would like to publicly acknowledge and thank a few people for their role in changing my life's direction and the effect it has had on me and this unique project on which I had the privilege of working for more than four decades.

As the first woman test pilot in Australia and a recipient of the Nancy-Bird Walton Memorial Trophy - the most prestigious award given by the Australian Women Pilots' Association, you would guess that Sciona Browne is an extraordinary person.

I should also mention that she took a leave of absence to star in the first Australian Survivor reality television show. It was filmed over three months on the Eyre Peninsula near the Great Australian Bight.

It was no surprise to us that, at the age of 50, she was runner-up to a former AFL player Rob Dickson - then Hawthorn's team runner. That might be considered more than remarkable but running up and down the 242 steps of Jacob's Ladder at King's Park half a dozen times every Saturday as Sciona did preparing for that adventure is not something I would aspire to.

The reason for mentioning this is that Sciona was also very perceptive. With the Foundation considering appointment of a full-time CEO, unbeknown to me she approached Bill Ross, the Foundation's elder statesman with a suggestion. In my absence, he convened a Board meeting resulting in an approach to me.

Before proceeding with our CEO search, would I be interested in taking a pay cut to become full-time Executive Chairman instead of devoting half my time on the Foundation's business in a voluntary capacity?

The timing was right. Following a second health scare the previous year that had seen me spend some time in an Intensive Care Unit after major surgery, I had been giving some thought to my priorities. After discussion with my wife of nearly 40 years and my business partner and, with only a couple of projects in the pipeline that Bruce could pursue, we agreed to wind down our business.

I accepted the role. This involved a move to Albany to live at the whaling station to plan the next 20+ years of development for the iconic attraction.

So, I have a lot to thank Sciona Browne, Bruce Gallash and the Board of The Jaycees Community Foundation Inc. for. It was a very satisfying three years of my life.

The plan evolved into the creation of the *Albany Biodiversity Park* on the site's degraded bushland as part of a sustainable, multi-faceted, three and a half million-dollar, tourism precinct.

It boasts Australian native animals and regional wildflowers, a 2,000-seat grassed amphitheatre and introduction of solar power. The only item not yet completed (but only for the want of a benefactor) is a subterranean eco-village and conference centre.

Timing is Everything | Peter J Snow OAM

Walken Djet (or rainbow flower) living mural is part of a unique regional wildflower garden presenting 80% of the flora on the south coast. It was inspired by Chateau de Villandry fruit and vegetable mural in France and Butchart Gardens in Canada.

Timing is Everything | Peter J Snow OAM

An *Australian Wildlife Park* features many species of native animals - making it a very popular attraction for families and international visitors. Additional features have been added as revenue or grants permitted. These include the "A Day in the Life of a Whaler" reflected image Spectravision unit, other technology-based exhibits, interpretative signage and access to the engine room of the Cheynes IV.

Other exhibits include the donated Hilda Hotker Collection of sea-shells displayed in the John Bell Gallery.

Probably the most significant exhibit is the Art of Scrimshaw featuring the extraordinary work of Gary Tonkin - regarded as the world's greatest living scrimshander – on a jaw-bone and 22 teeth of one of the largest whales caught off Albany.

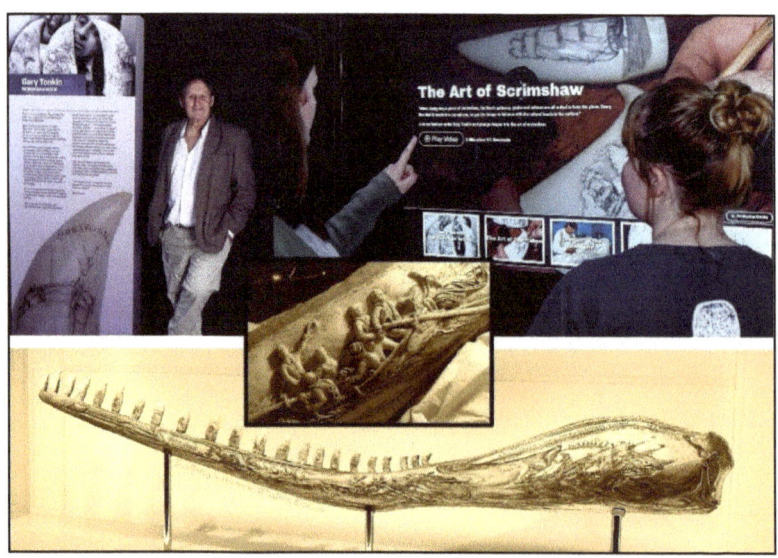

Timing is Everything | Peter J Snow OAM

The project has not been without its obstacles. Apart from the tragic aircraft accident death of our manager of 16 years, the late John Bell, one big challenge turned into litigation.

This was related to a $1.3 million breakwater and landing facility to allow vessels to bring passengers directly to the site via water. Despite multiple reports that permitted construction to proceed, a fundamental error had occurred. On completion, the landing platform area very quickly filled with sand - preventing local operators delivering the expected thousands of visitors by boat.

Timing is Everything | Peter J Snow OAM

It appeared that wave modelling had been limited to waves from one direction. This was an Ocean Engineering 1.01 basic error.

Having not been involved until the construction stage, the Foundation had no contractual right of action to sue. At the recommendation of the principal of local firm, Latro Lawyers, a Supreme Court action for "not-fit-for-purpose" negligence was commenced against the two multi-national consultancies involved in the wave modelling and engineering.

It was to be a David vs Goliath action ... but like the outcome of the biblical tale, the Foundation received a significant out-of-court settlement. Unfortunately, the cost of reparation would be more than the original project cost. With the compensation inadequate to deliver the intended outcome, the funds were applied to other development projects on the site.

Today, there is a pristine sheltered beach, but no passenger landing platform. Amazing that the absence of one additional professional report costing a few thousand dollars can destroy a million-dollar project!

It also proved that despite herculean opposition with unlimited resources, a minnow can beat a whale - if you have right and fairness on your side and are prepared to be persistent.

Perhaps sending the Chairman of the reluctant respondent copies of the Foundation's annual reports with photos of the disaster and referring to corporate social responsibility may have prompted their anxiety to settle the unfortunate predicament.

Timing is Everything | Peter J Snow OAM

The project has, and continues to receive many museum, heritage and tourism awards.

These are tributes to the many volunteers who put so much time and effort into creating a unique, iconic heritage attraction.

Deserving special recognition are - *Les Bail* who offered three months help after John Bell's tragic death in 1996.

He stayed for 13 years - overseeing the major restoration program - and the development of Albany Biodiversity Park.

Glenn Russell succeeded Les as General Manager and retired to become chair of *Discovery Bay Tourism Precinct Ltd* which now operates the site.

And finally, the Bell family, John, Jill and their sons, Peter and Jamie, whose ingenuity and artistic skills are evident in many of the exhibits and displays.

Timing is Everything | Peter J Snow OAM

With the assistance of state, federal, Lotterywest grants and private donors, visitor admission revenue and merchandise sales, it is now one of the region's premier attractions.

PROUDLY SUPPORTED BY

THE GREEN FAMILY
THE JACK FAMILY CHARITABLE TRUST

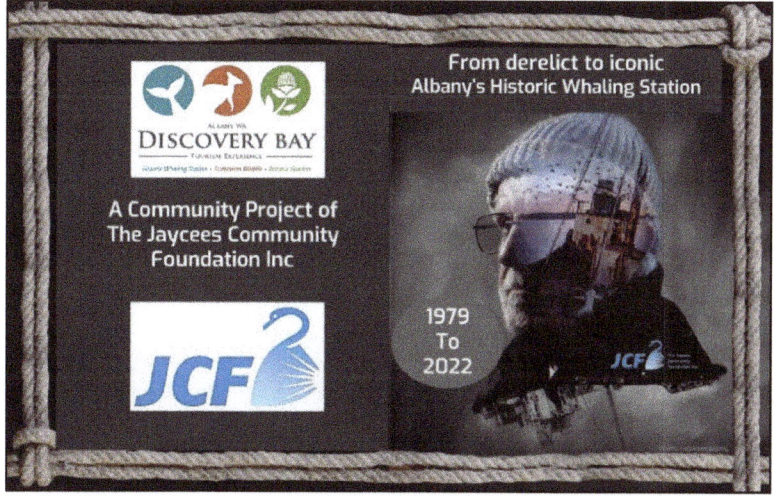

One might say of this amazing adventure: *"right place, right time"* or, better still: *"Timing is Everything"*.

Timing is Everything | Peter J Snow OAM

POSTSCRIPT: As part of its long-term plan, the Foundation handed over responsibility for the award-winning heritage tourism icon to the local community in 2023 – after more than two million visitors and a contribution of more than $40 million to the local economy.

This was achieved in a way not originally planned when it was realised that a transfer of the assets to a new sole purpose not-for-profit entity would incur more than $175,000 in transfer duty.

Instead, the name of The Jaycees Community Foundation Inc was changed to *Albany Heritage Foundation Inc* and a new local Board appointed. The Foundation is sole member of Discovery Bay Tourism Precinct Ltd which operates the business.

LESSONS:
1. IMPOSSIBLE DREAMS ARE POSSIBLE.
2, DON'T LET REALITY INHIBIT VISION.
3. A LOAD SHARED MAKES THE LOAD DISPROPORTIONALLY LIGHTER.
4. DETERMINATION AND PERSISTENCE CAN OVERCOME MOST OBSTACLES.
5. NEVER CEASE THE SEARCH FOR EXCELLENCE AND INNOVATION.

MORE BY THE AUTHOR

What do a business co-founder, a foster carer of 220 babies, Australia's "unluckiest" AFL player, an alpaca breeder, and a fire chief have in common? A love of a football club—and extraordinary stories of resilience and achievement.
The Tribe: Volume 1 shares 15 inspiring tales of everyday people proving greatness often lies in the ordinary. From a lolly-pop Santa to Western Australia's most decorated footballer, these diverse stories celebrate community, courage, and passion. Introduced by someone who knows them all, this collection highlights the power of shared purpose and connection. Be inspired by their journeys and discover what extraordinary truly means.

The Tribe: Volume 2 celebrates 15 more remarkable individuals connected through a football club. These inspiring stories reveal how passion, determination, and community spirit drive extraordinary achievements.
From a bush bank manager to a Serbian rugby player, a school principal, a mother of four, a CEO, a business founder, each story showcases resilience and the power of community. Whether building careers, transforming communities, or overcoming challenges, these individuals prove greatness is within reach for us all.
Be inspired by **The Tribe: Volume 2** and discover what's possible with connection and courage.

Discover the inspiring stories of 15 remarkable individuals who dared to dream, persevere, and make an impact.
Movers & Shakers shares semi-biographical snapshots of everyday heroes excelling in the commercial, community, and personal arenas. From career reinventions that launched award-winning businesses to contributions that transformed communities, these stories showcase the power of resilience, creativity, and purpose. Each journey reveals what it takes to overcome challenges, embrace opportunities, and make the world a better place. Whether you're seeking motivation for your own ambitions or inspiration from others' achievements, **Movers & Shakers** will leave you empowered and ready to act.

For more information on release dates, availability or contact with the Author scan the QR code at right or email
snow.jcf@gmail.com

www.ingramcontent.com/pod-product-compliance
Lightning Source LLC
Chambersburg PA
CBHW062037290426
44109CB00026B/2648